"With Kurt's book Pure Food, he proves that healthy, well-sourced food doesn't have to compromise on flavor."
—TOM COLICCHIO, CHEF/OWNER OF CRAFT RESTAURANTS, FOOD POLICY ACTIVIST, AND HEAD JUDGE ON *TOP CHEF*

"This spectacular cookbook reflects all the passion and joy Kurt puts into feeding people. Pure Food will inspire chefs and enliven meals everywhere."
—ETHAN STOWELL, CHEF/OWNER OF ETHAN STOWELL RESTAURANTS, AUTHOR, AND MULTIPLE JAMES BEARD AWARD–NOMINEE FOR BEST CHEF: NORTHWEST

"Part personal story, part treatise on 'real' food, and part cookbook; this book sucks you into Kurt's story, makes your mouth water, and teaches you all at once. . . . Read this book—shop—cook with your family, and then sit down at the table and enjoy!"
—ANN COOPER, CHEF, AUTHOR, AND FOUNDER OF THE CHEF ANN FOUNDATION

"No matter what your dietary stripes, this beautiful book gives you the tools to ditch processed foods, and instead source quality ingredients and cook clean healthy foods with mind-blowing flavors."
—TESS MASTERS, AUTHOR OF *THE BLENDER GIRL* AND *THE BLENDER GIRL SMOOTHIES*

"Let's follow Kurt's lead and insist on truthful, pure foods and at the same time make our dinner tables tastier, healthier, and full of integrity!"
—TOM DOUGLAS, JAMES BEARD AWARD–WINNER, CHEF, RESTAURATEUR, AUTHOR, AND RADIO HOST

Pure Food

# Kurt Beecher Dammeier

# Pure Food

A Chef's Handbook for
EATING CLEAN
with Healthy,
Delicious Recipes

Photography by Barnard & Meyer

BenBella

DALLAS, TX

My goal with this book is to make cooking as user-friendly and foolproof as possible while still being super tasty. So, you'll see that throughout the book I've written in notes and tips (yes, that's my own writing, not some generic handwriting font!) where I think a little extra guidance could make a difference. I hope you find these helpful.

BenBella Books, Inc.
PO Box 572028
Dallas, TX 75357
www.benbellabooks.com
Send feedback to feedback@benbellabooks.com

Printed in Korea
10 9 8 7 6 5 4 3 2 1

Library of Congress Cataloging-in-Publication Data is available upon request.
LCCN: 2015039197
ISBN-13: 978-1-942952-17-6

Editing by Heather Butterfield
Copyediting by Karen Levy
Proofreading by Kimberly Broderick
Indexing by Clive Pyne Book Indexing Services
Text design and composition by Alicia Nammacher

Cover design by Alicia Nammacher
Photography by Barnard & Meyer
Photos on pages 10, 11, 13, and 26–28
    by Erinn J. Hale, Beecher's
    Pure Food Kids Foundation

Distributed by Perseus Distribution
www.perseusdistribution.com

To place orders through Perseus Distribution:
Tel: (800) 343-4499
Fax: (800) 351-5073
E-mail: orderentry@perseusbooks.com

Significant discounts for bulk sales are available.
Please contact Aida Herrera at aida@benbellabooks.com.

CURRIED LEG OF LAMB WITH ROASTED GRAPE SALSA AND SPICY CHICKPEA PUREE

BEEF AND
PEPERONATA
CROSTINI

To my mother, Janet, who was my original inspiration to cook, and to my wife, Leslie, who is my everyday customer.

Although my mother has been gone for twelve years and I've been married to Leslie for twenty-four, these two continue to be the most important people in my life.

# Acknowledgments

Many people were instrumental in putting this book together, but five people are at the top of the list: Sharon Bowers, my agent who helped me assemble this team; Elizabeth Dunn, who co-wrote the text; Julie Riendl, who honcho'd the entire project; Celeste Rogers, who worked with me in my NYC apartment developing the recipes; and although she didn't work much on this book, my longtime recipe wingman, Lura Smith. A special thank you to all our recipe testers, corralled by Amy Nygaard, who provided important feedback throughout: Tonya Bautista, Melody Burson, Julia Crain, Theresa Edwards, Lucy Ellis, Bob and Sue Frause, Rachel and Rob Hartley, Whitney Heinrich, Christine Hill Moore, Adele Hoople, Ken Iliffe, Rachel Katz-Carey, Tomi Kent-Smith, Alison Leber, Ben Libby and Lauren Caster, Michael Lonsdale, Caitlin McAloney, Lindsey McDowell, Molly Olsen, Katrina Ooms, Cassie Pehl, Suzanne Poole, and Donna Werner.

# Contents

OLD BAY ROASTED
TURKEY BREAST.
OPPOSITE PAGE:
UPPER EAST SIDE
STEAK SAUCE

# Introduction

If only my 50-year-old self could go back in time to make this soup for my 24-yr-old self...

HEARTY
CHICKEN
SOUP

## MY PURE FOOD CRUSADE STARTED WITH A HEAD COLD.

I was 24 years old and working as a sales rep for my family's printing company. Our office was in Seattle's Fremont neighborhood, way before it was hip. At that time, back in the '80s, we shared the area with light industrial businesses and marine stores, which meant the lunch options were no great shakes. There were a couple of crappy delis and a fish and chips shop. And then there was a Chinese restaurant. It had a dimly lit dining room with an orange shag carpet and Naugahyde booths, and an attached cocktail lounge where there were always a few heavy drinkers nursing screwdrivers and tequila sunrises. This was the sort of place that served all the usual staples

of Westernized Szechuan cuisine: Kung Pao chicken, beef lo mein, fortune cookies, and my personal favorite, hot and sour soup. There were probably a thousand just like it scattered across the U.S.

One day I detected the beginnings of a nasty cold, and I got it into my head that hot and sour soup would be the best thing for it. Like most people, I thought of soups in general as wholesome and nourishing fare—the stuff of Jewish grandmothers and Campbell's commercials—and I had this idea that garlic and hot pepper might have some kind of curative properties for a cold. So, off I went to the neighborhood Chinese restaurant for a big bowl of hot and sour soup.

When I woke up the next day I felt even worse than I had the day before, like someone had taken a jackhammer to my head. Again, at lunch, I went for a bowl of hot and sour soup, hoping that another helping of the warm, comforting broth would do the trick. Again, the following day I woke up feeling worse. Five days into my hot and sour soup cure, I felt like I had a brain tumor. I couldn't even be near light. It was at that point that somebody I worked with innocently asked the question that I now realize should have been so obvious to me: was it possible that I was allergic to MSG? Because, well, there was probably MSG in the soup.

I didn't even know what MSG was, much less whether I was allergic to it. It was the first time in my life I considered the idea that food could be bad for you.

It's hard to believe now, when there is so much healthy skepticism over where our food comes from and what's inside, that I could have been so naive. But I grew up at a time when it was virtually unthinkable that big companies, under the U.S. government's watch, could give you anything to eat that was bad for you. Those were the days before the Watergate scandal and the Vietnam War backlash cracked the armor of trust in American institutions, and these were our most respected establishments. If the federal government deemed something fit for consumption, well, then, it must be safe to eat. I don't remember any discussions during my youth about health and food, aside from the ones pertaining to weight loss. There was positively no skepticism on the subject of food additives and what they might be doing to us.

For my generation and for my parents' generation, science held the promise of solving the "problem" of food. There wasn't this general sense we have today that food and its pursuit could be a leisure activity, a source of enjoyment; food was fuel, and the good scientists at General Mills and Kraft and Nestlé were working hard to make it faster and easier to prepare—not to mention cheaper and tastier. That was back when the word "organic" meant dirty and primitive, not "premium" as it does today. I like to call this the Tangification of the American diet. Tang, that artificial foodstuff that uses synthetic ingredients to recreate the flavor of orange juice (with almost none of the health benefits), was the poster child for this way of thinking. I remember when it was on the news that astronauts, our national heroes, were taking Tang into space—not that old-fashioned stuff squeezed from oranges. Better living through chemistry!

> I don't remember any discussions during my youth about health and food, aside from the ones pertaining to weight loss. There was positively no skepticism on the subject of food additives and what they might be doing to us.

So here I was in my twenties, considering for the first time that someone had added something to my food that had the power to make me sick. Sure enough, as soon as I laid off the soup, my symptoms went away and I returned to good health. So what was this MSG thing, and how had it ended up in my soup?

I started doing my research and learned that MSG stands for monosodium glutamate, an industrially produced salt of an amino acid that is added to foods to enhance their flavor. And MSG isn't just found in cheap Chinese food, like my hot and sour soup: you'll find it on fast food menus and in supermarket items like canned soups, salad dressings, ramen noodles, Doritos, and many, many others. MSG is a quick, cheap way to turbo-charge flavor, so you better believe that food processors take ample advantage of it.

MSG was discovered in 1908 when the Japanese scientist Ikeda Kikunae got to thinking about why dashi, the broth made from dried seaweed and fish, was so rich in flavor. Through experiments on the seaweed used in making dashi, Ikeda was able to isolate the white, crystalline compound responsible for the broth's meaty, savory flavor: $C_5H_9NO_4$, or glutamic acid. He added a sodium molecule to this compound to make monosodium glutamate and began selling the pale powder under the brand name Ajinomoto as a food additive designed to enhance flavor. Ikeda's monosodium glutamate came from seaweed, but these days, MSG is made by fermenting starch, sugar beets, sugarcane, or molasses.

Although Ikeda initially saw MSG as a miracle ingredient capable of making healthy ingredients tastier (and therefore more enticing), its uses over the past 100 years have proven far less constructive. Put simply, adding MSG helps food processors reduce the amount of "real" ingredients in their foods. Period. Why use large quantities of expensive beef or chicken to flavor broth when the addition of MSG will mimic the meaty flavor at a tiny fraction of the price?

If you look up MSG in *Food Additives: A Shopper's Guide to What's Safe & What's Not*, here's what you'll find:

MSG: aka Accent, Aginomoto, Natural Meat Tenderizer; mutagen; causes obesity; addictive, makes you eat more; may cause diabetes, migraines, headaches, itching, nausea, brain, nervous system, reproductive disorders, high blood pressure, Autism, ADHD, Alzheimer's, retina damage, blindness; pregnant, lactating mothers, infants, small children should avoid; allergic reactions common; generally produced using GMO bacteria; may be derived from corn.

### AWAKENED TO ALL THIS NEW INFORMATION ABOUT MSG—

not only its potential to cause allergic reactions, but also its common usage in covering up for substandard ingredients—I started avoiding foods with MSG in them wherever I could. I found that this was almost impossible to do at restaurants, where there was no requirement to disclose the use of food additives, and few were likely to volunteer information that undercut the quality of their food. Soon, I also discovered that foods without MSG listed on their label were making me feel unwell in much the same way I experienced from the hot and sour soup.

Confused, I dove into research again, and discovered another troubling fact about MSG: an FDA loophole allowed food processors to list it on their labels under many, many different names. Glutamic acid, whey protein, gelatin, yeast extract, and autolyzed yeast were just a few of the many monikers that MSG could hide under in an ingredient list. Often food packages would tout "No MSG!" or "No added MSG!" while containing processed free glutamic acid, which is essentially the same thing. As a result, MSG was hidden in products ranging from some infant formulas and chewing gum to protein bars. The amount of MSG used was never listed— it wasn't required by the FDA—which made it impossible to know just what kind of a dose I was getting.

Today, almost thirty years after my hot and sour soup revelation, MSG is still hiding in plain sight on ingredient lists and people are still arguing over whether it's harmful. The FDA still classifies MSG as "GRAS" — Generally Recognized as Safe—a designation that means that the agency has "reviewed,"

I grew up at a time when it was virtually unthinkable that big companies, under the U.S. government's watch, could give you anything to eat that was bad for you.

but not formally approved, the safety of the substance (more on that whole train wreck in A Short History of Processed Food, page 17). Food manufacturers today are still free to put MSG in their foods in whatever quantity they like.

Studies have shown that some people are sensitive to large amounts of MSG, reacting as I did with headaches, nausea, and weakness. In certain cases, they also complain of wheezing, changes in heart rate, and difficulty breathing. Others have demonstrated that MSG can cause weight gain. But the science on MSG is still inconclusive, with the research showing contradictory findings. There are many—including current "it" chef David Chang—who support the use of MSG, on the basis that the lab-made powder is chemically identical to a substance that occurs in nature. Glutamate is a common amino acid, found naturally in nearly all foods and in particularly high levels in items like tomatoes, mushrooms, and Parmesan cheese. The human body also produces glutamate, where it plays an essential role as a neurotransmitter.

The fact that glutamate occurs in nature doesn't mean that when it is produced industrially and dispensed in overlarge quantities, isolated from its ordinary biological context, it's just as safe as the stuff you find in Roquefort cheese. Glutamates that occur naturally in food come packaged alongside a whole host of different nutrients that may help the body to regulate and manage their metabolism. Nature is full of these complex relationships between nutrients, and our understanding of their significance is still evolving. Take, for example, iron: popping an iron supplement isn't nearly as effective as getting it from spinach or red meat. When it comes to biochemistry, context is everything.

The current debate over food additives—and their presumed safety unless otherwise proven unsafe—puts me in mind of another major public health crisis. Although it's hard to believe now, it wasn't until as recently as the 1960s, after more than a hundred years of widespread general use, that cigarettes were widely accepted as dangerous. For decades the government told people that cigarettes were safe. They were recommended by doctors as calming and beneficial to digestion. Professional baseball players endorsed them in print and radio ads. Tobacco was a plant, after all—how could it be bad for you? The government didn't officially come out against cigarettes until 1964, in the form of a Surgeon General's Report, which was far too late for the hundreds of thousands of people who had succumbed to their poison. I believe that food additives will chart a similar course.

So while today there may be no good scientific consensus on the safety of MSG and the thousands of other additives crammed into our food, I firmly believe that deep down, we know that eating food that's filled with industrial powders isn't good for us. Our intuition tells us this. You don't feel as good after eating additive-laden foods as you do after eating pure, unadulterated ones. Back in the '80s, I didn't need a whole bunch of studies to tell me that I should avoid MSG as best I could. You have two choices: you can wait for the science to catch up to what you already instinctively know, or you can take the artificial stuff out of your life now.

## I'VE GONE ON AT LENGTH ABOUT ALL OF MY ISSUES WITH MSG,

but in truth, monosodium glutamate is just the tip of the iceberg, one of thousands of additives in the toxic chemical stew that we call our modern food supply. It is hardly the most toxic. My nasty run-in with MSG happened to be what ignited a fuse in me when it came to removing food additives from my life, but the problem goes far, far deeper.

By the mid-'90s, foods were rapidly becoming more heavily adulterated, and my allergies started kicking in with a wider array of foods. Foods that I had never had any issues with began bothering me. I started to have headaches and sinus problems. I felt lethargic all the time. I started reading ingredient labels religiously, and realized that foods that I considered to be simple, wholesome fare—so-called "whole wheat" sandwich bread, energy bars, yogurts—often had ingredient lists a mile long and filled with substances that sounded like they belonged in a chemistry lab rather than a kitchen. For all their claims of healthfulness, these foods were anything but. I cut many of them out of my life, challenging myself to eat packaged foods only when necessary, and only ones without added chemicals at that. I started to feel better.

In 1998 my family sold our printing business and I began looking for my next act in life. I loved food and was committed to starting another family business, so I bought Pasta & Co—a local Seattle food shop that sold prepared foods and gourmet grocery items. Pasta & Co was then, and still is now, generally regarded as selling the highest-quality deli food in Seattle, so getting back in their kitchens and seeing where their ingredients came from was a wake-up call in terms of just how many additives are used in restaurants (even really good restaurants). We've made big changes to Pasta & Co since then, but at the time, what I saw really horrified me.

Take French fries: I don't know if I imagined that all restaurants were peeling, cutting, and frying theirs from scratch, but once I realized they arrived frozen in bags from some factory, coated with chemical flavorings, it was eye-opening in terms of how much goes on behind the scenes that we would never imagine as diners.

Given that I had dedicated myself to removing additives from my own life, I knew that Pasta & Co needed to start walking my talk. When I had the discussion with all of

> I firmly believe that deep down, we know that eating food that's filled with industrial powders isn't good for us. Our intuition tells us this.

my people about removing food additives from the menu, there was a lot of initial resistance. We had to change 173 recipes so that they no longer contained commercial soup base, bottled lemon juice, Worcestershire sauce, pre-made salad dressings, preservative-laden bread. Plus, anything we were selling that contained additives had to go: cilantro chutney, golden raisins, bottled lemonade, et cetera. It was an immense task and it cost us a lot more to operate this way. But I think if you ask anybody who was involved in that transition, they would tell you that they feel proud of all that we've accomplished and the way we do business today.

After purchasing Pasta & Co, my next ambition was to start a food brand from scratch. I loved cheese and had realized that there was virtually no American artisan cheese in Seattle (at that time, in 2002, there was very little artisan cheese anywhere in the U.S.). So I founded Beecher's Handmade Cheese, named to honor my great-grandfather Beecher. I wanted Beecher's to stand for something; that led to forming the Beecher's Pure Food Kids Foundation, which used 1% of sales from the company to educate schoolchildren about how to be savvier consumers of processed foods (more information on the foundation follows in the next chapter).

In 2006 I wrote a cookbook, *Pure Flavor*,

and figured that if I was going to put together 125 recipes, I might as well open a restaurant where I could serve them. That became Bennett's, a casual bistro with ingredients deeply rooted in the Cascadia region, an area extending from northern California to southern Alaska, and the coast to the continental divide, taking in Washington, most of Oregon and Idaho, and part of Montana. Next I opened Maximus/Minimus—a food truck in the shape of a pig, serving pulled pork sandwiches. Who said pure food can't also be fun?

Since then, I've expanded Beecher's to New York City, opened another casual bistro in Seattle called Liam's, and bought a Wagyu beef company called Mishima Reserve. My company's name is Sugar Mountain, an homage to the Neil Young song about an amusement park of the same name. "You can't be twenty on Sugar Mountain," as the song goes. If you're having fun, you won't grow old.

Sugar Mountain is always growing and changing, and what underpins it all is a commitment to offering up pure, full-flavored, additive-free food.

Today, I'm happy to say I live my life additive-free (well, almost additive free; nobody's perfect). My businesses make food from scratch, the hard way, without any of the white powdered substances that go into so much of the food that's out there these days. I still miss my MSG-laden Worcestershire sauce sometimes, and from time to time it's tedious to have to squeeze lemons and limes for marinades and cocktails rather than buying the pre-juiced versions peppered with sodium benzoate and other preservatives. Mostly, though, eating pure is just a part of my life. I don't think about it anymore.

I'm writing this book for the same reason I started Beecher's Handmade Cheese, revamped the way we do business at Pasta & Co, and founded my Beecher's Pure Food Kids Foundation: to help change the way we eat in America. The goal of this book is to arm families with the tools they need to cut additives from their lives.

I've found through personal experience that if there's one thing you can do above all else to take your health into your own hands, it's learning to cook for yourself and your loved ones. It's not hard, but it does require commitment. It means spending a little more at the grocery store to get quality ingredients, planning your meals further in advance, and logging some extra time at the stove. But you'll be richly rewarded with that warm feeling that comes from feeding your family right. And in how you feel, day in and day out.

Kurt

FOR THIS PURE FOOD KIDS
EASY-TO-MAKE RECIPE,
GO TO PUREFOODKIDS.ORG.

Pure Food Kids

THIS BOOK IS GEARED TOWARD HELPING ADULTS REMOVE ADDITIVES FROM THEIR DIETS BY CHANGING THE WAY THEY SHOP, COOK, AND EAT. BUT LONG BEFORE I GOT INTERESTED IN TALKING TO PEOPLE MY OWN AGE ABOUT HOW TO EAT FOR BETTER HEALTH, MY FIRST PASSION WAS TEACHING THESE LESSONS TO KIDS.

Shortly after Beecher's Handmade Cheese opened for business in 2003, I turned my attention from how we were going to make money to how we were going to give it away. Beecher's carries a family name (my middle name), and I wanted the business to stand for something. By that point in my life, I was 100 percent livid about the tactics that I saw food manufacturers using to hook children on heavily processed foods that would only make them sick and overweight. I knew that I wanted to devote a portion of our sales to educating kids to cope with all the marketing they're exposed to, and teaching them a healthy sense of skepticism when it comes to their food choices.

In the beginning, I imagined that we would simply find a good charity and donate extensively to their efforts. After a year of looking, though, we realized that there was nobody out there doing the kind of work we had in mind. So, we decided that we would take on the challenge ourselves. We started the Beecher's Pure Food Kids Foundation in 2004.

Our mission was, and is, simple: to arm kids with the knowledge and skills they need to make healthy food choices. We want to change the way America eats. Food companies are formidable adversaries, spending more than $2 billion each year marketing industrial food to children, and we believe

that children need tools to recognize and resist the sophisticated and often misleading claims and tactics large corporations use to sell their products. Kids also need nutrition knowledge and label-reading skills to identify the potential health dangers in what they're being sold.

Our strategy was based on my own childhood remembrances of the anti-smoking campaign that came into my fifth grade classroom. After seeing a gruesome video of a smoker with a tracheotomy hole and learning about the dangers of the habit, I went home and made life difficult for my parents, who were both smokers. I remembered how brutally effective that single classroom visit was, not only in terms of my own health, but the health of my whole family. I wanted to pattern our nutritional education on that approach.

We knew off the bat we would focus on fourth and fifth graders. Ten- and eleven-year-olds are young enough to be interested and engaged, but old enough to be able to read, write, and do the simple math required to determine, say, the total grams of sugar in a box of Frosted Flakes. This is an age where kids are very receptive to new information, and studies show that they retain it well. Middle and high schoolers will be much more rebellious and less inclined to take guidance on their diet from authority figures. Adults are even worse; they are the least receptive to changing their food behaviors. Our theory is that ten- and eleven-year-olds can be the most effective change agents for the whole family.

The goal was to spark change in these kids, and get them curious enough about their food choices to start asking more questions and influencing the way their parents shop. Hopefully, they would begin to understand the power of where they spend their food dollars, and ultimately put demand-side pressure on food manufacturers to produce cleaner food.

I enlisted my friend Alison Leber for help. Neither of us had backgrounds in education, so the first thing we did was approach Washington State University and ask them to develop a curriculum with us. They already had a class up and running with some similar elements, but their approach was to go into low-income schools and spend weeks creating a school garden. We were looking for a more tactical, in-and-out approach that would let us provide basic food label literacy to the maximum number of kids, something that would go an inch deep and a mile wide.

Working with WSU as well as various outside educators and nutritionists, we put

together a curriculum for a two-and-a-half-hour workshop that we felt covered all of the most important facts about making responsible food choices, without burying the kids in too much information. Our first workshops were in 2006. We started on Mercer Island, which is where my kids were in school, and expanded from there, with Alison and me teaching the workshops ourselves.

Since then, we've taught almost 90,000 students how to be "food detectives," reading labels and investigating packaged foods to understand their nutritional content. Today, we employ five full-time staff members as well as fourteen part-time instructors, and reach 15,000 kids a year between New York City and Seattle.

We cover a lot of ground in our two and a half hours in the classroom. First, we teach students what "marketing" means and how food companies lie to them, using cartoons and bright colors to lure them in, as well as certain images and health claims to convince them the food is more nutritious than it is. We bring in real products for them to inspect: Yoplait, Cheetos, Froot Loops, Vitaminwater, Powerade, Gushers. We don't pull any punches and we try to make the lessons as applicable to their real-world food decisions as possible.

After looking at the words and images on the front of the food package, the next step is to teach them where to find the truth about whether the product is everything it's cracked up to be. That means reading nutrition labels. We talk about how to understand serving size and whether it's realistic—for instance, we show them that there are nine servings in one medium bag of Cheetos, which means that Cheetos is pretending for nutrition label purposes that you're sharing your snack with eight friends. A bottle of Powerade has two and a half servings, which means you're supposed to share it with one and a half friends (the kids always crack up at that line).

We do a big focus on sugars, and have amped up that portion of the workshop over time. It's out of control how much sugar is hiding in processed foods and drinks; many kids get three or four times more added sugar daily than they need. So, we have kids do the math themselves to figure out how much sugar is in the entire package, and translate that into sugar cubes to help them visualize those grams of sugar.

We teach them about ingredient lists, and how they're organized from the highest weight ingredient to the lowest weight ingredient. So, if you're looking at a bag of Cheetos and cheese is the number 25 ingredient, it means there isn't very much cheese in them at all. Is the food's ingredient list long or short? Short means fewer than five ingredients, and those foods tend to be healthier. Longer ingredient lists mean you are eating a highly processed food.

Can you picture all the ingredients in your head? If not, it's a good sign that they are chemical additives. Does the flavor advertised on the front of the package actually appear on the ingredient list? If a drink is strawberry-kiwi flavored, strawberries and kiwis should be on the ingredient list, right?

The final element of the workshop is to turn kids into "chefs" and work as a group to cook a basic vegetarian chili. Our instructors arrive in classrooms armed with a hot plate, ingredients, cutting boards, and safety knives. Adults who view cooking as a chore might be surprised to hear that the opportunity to cook is the highlight of the workshop for most kids. It's the big payoff we use to motivate them to get through the information at the beginning. Kids love getting in on the action, chopping and slicing and seeing how it all comes together, and most of all, tasting something they made with their own two hands.

The Pure Food Kids workshops are as much

Since 2006, we've taught almost 90,000 students how to be "food detectives," reading labels and investigating packaged foods to understand their nutritional content.

about what we do as what we don't do. We're not trying to give the kids an encyclopedic knowledge of food additives; we're just trying to spark their curiosity so that they'll read a label the next time they buy a bag of Fritos at the convenience store after school, or go shopping with their parents. The key lesson here is rather than try to make people into food scientists who can identify every single additive, it's better to stick with a few simple rules that they can follow and remember.

And, we're realists. We don't expect kids to walk out of the workshop, throw away their Fruit by the Foot, and start eating vegetables all day long. What we're trying to do is empower them to make a healthier real-world choice, even if that choice is Kettle Chips instead of Flamin' Hot Cheetos.

Of course, Beecher's Pure Foods Kids Foundation is one of many organizations focused on the dire position of our nation's children. Today, almost one in five children are obese. Kids are succumbing to diseases like type 2 diabetes and liver damage, previously seen only in adults. The state of our children's weight is a public health crisis, and it's quite clear that overly sugar- and chemical-laden diets and sedentary lifestyles are to blame. Concerned citizens all over America are finding ways to reach kids and improve their health.

In the past decade, there have been many different attempts to tackle nutrition in a school setting. It makes sense. Schools are where children from all backgrounds spend the majority of their time, and many children eat two of their three daily meals there.

Schools should be role models for good behavior, nutritional and otherwise. Efforts at school lunch reform aim to strengthen the nutritional requirements for the food served in cafeterias, along with increasing their federal funding, updating kitchen facilities, and installing salad bars. Some programs, such as Wellness in the Schools (WITS) in New York, have gone as far as encouraging chefs to "adopt" a school, working behind the scenes to transform its lunch program. School garden initiatives like Alice Waters's Edible Schoolyard involve children growing their own food in a special plot of land at school, in an attempt to ignite their interest in fresh fruits and vegetables. They all contribute to the critical goal of getting our kids off on the right foot when it comes to their eating habits.

Likewise, for parents reading this chapter at home: you can, and should, do what you can to turn your kids into food detectives. The Beecher's Pure Food Kids workshop and programs like it currently reach only a fraction of America's school kids. You as parents can take the lead in helping your kids combat food marketing today. Harness their natural curiosity to get them reading labels. Play "Where's Waldo?" with the word "hydrogenated," which indicates trans fat. Challenge them to use their math skills to figure out how many sugar cubes are in that bowl of cereal. Get them in on the action to help prepare dinner. You might be surprised by how much fun they have. Before long, you'll find that they're the ones scanning the grocery cart for clean labels.

*[handwritten margin note: Real change has to happen in the real world— not just farm to table.]*

PAN-ROASTED CHICKEN BREASTS

# A Short History of Processed Food

HUMANS HAVE BEEN PROCESSING FOOD FOR EONS, MILLING GRAIN AND BAKING IT INTO BREAD AND SALTING OR DRYING MEATS TO STRETCH OUT THEIR USEFUL LIFE. Milk was made into cheese; grain fermented into beer; vegetables packed in vinegar for pickles; pork bellies smoked to make bacon; olives pressed for their oil. For 10,000 years, that was about the extent of it when it came to doctoring foods and protecting them for storage. Then in the twentieth century, our diets began to change in a radical way, thanks (or no thanks) to advances in science and manufacturing.

In my own lifetime, I've witnessed a public health implosion in the United States. I don't think that's an overstatement. Obesity rates have more than doubled in adults since the 1960s and tripled in children since the 1980s. Today, more than one in three adults is obese, and as previously mentioned, almost one in five children. Nearly 10 percent of the population now has type 2 diabetes. This and other diet-related conditions, such as heart disease, stroke, and certain types of cancer, are some of the leading causes of preventable death in the United States.

Meanwhile, the major institutions that we once trusted implicitly have been exposed. For decades, the government and big corporations have peddled misguided nutritional guidance that has wound up making us fatter, every time (think back to the war on animal fats, then carbohydrates, and now gluten). Now, for the first time in two centuries, the current generation of children in America may have shorter life expectancies than their parents. The estimated medical cost of obesity in this country is around $150 billion per year. This is serious stuff. As a country, we've grown fat and sedentary. We spend less and less of our time and money on cooking, and more of it visiting the doctor.

If all those facts and figures are hard to wrap your head around, try this exercise. Dig through your home for photographs of people from the 1960s or earlier. Take a look at what you see. What's different? Everybody is thinner. Bellies are flat, legs and arms spindly, cheekbones contoured. Bodies looked different in my childhood.

It's pretty startling when you think about it—that the shape of the average human frame could shift so dramatically from one generation to the next.

With apologies to Paleo dieters, I don't think we can blame the change on our transition to agriculture, which took place roughly 12,000 years ago. Advocates of raw food diets would do well to remember that we've been cooking with fire for roughly a million years, and

> As a country, we've grown fat and sedentary. We spend less and less of our time and money on cooking, and more of it visiting the doctor.

haven't been worse for wear until recently. Folks who believe that veganism is the only path to good health might have trouble explaining the remarkably lithe, hearty physiques of committed carnivores like Africa's Masai and the nomads of Mongolia. The major change to the American diet that coincided with the obesity epidemic? That was the advent of highly processed food, filled with chemicals to boost flavor and prolong shelf life.

What do I mean by "highly processed"? I like the definition offered by Melanie Warner, the journalist and author of *Pandora's Lunchbox*: "Something that could not be made, with the same ingredients, in a home kitchen." I'm not talking about salad that's been washed and bagged, frozen berries, pasteurized milk, or pork butchered from a single carcass into individual cuts, all of which are types of processing. I'm talking about food fabricated wholesale from corn sweeteners, preservatives, dyes, flavor enhancers, emulsifiers, thickeners, and gelling agents—food that my youthful self wouldn't recognize as food.

In just a few short decades, processing has evolved from minimally invasive kitchen counter activities like canning, salting, and drying to a highly technical, multibillion-dollar industry that can (and does) fabricate entire food items from the cheapest materials possible into highly addictive, shelf-stable fare. About 70 percent of the calories we eat today come from highly processed foods, foods that didn't

## LEADING CONTRIBUTORS TO PREMATURE DEATH 2010

| | |
|---|---|
| Diet | 678,000 |
| Tobacco | 465,000 |
| High blood pressure | 442,700 |
| High body-mass index | 364,000 |
| Physical inactivity | 234,000 |
| High total cholesterol | 158,400 |
| Alcohol and drug use | 111,000 |

(Numbers indicate premature deaths)

Source info: U.S Burden of Disease Collaborators (Murray CJL, et al.). "The State of U.S. Health, 1990–2010: Burden of Diseases, Injuries, and Risk Factors." *Journal of the American Medical Association* 2013, vol. 310, pp. s178–s179.

PURPLE POTATO
SALAD WITH
PEA VINES

even exist before the twentieth century.

Changing how we eat has also changed how much we eat. As of 2010, Americans consumed 60 percent more added fats and 25 percent more calories than we did in 1970. While total sugar consumption has risen, the real story is the changing way that sugar is delivered: in 1970, the average American consumed a third of a pound of high fructose corn syrup annually. Today, that number is around 26 pounds. It should come as no surprise that our national health is flagging and our waistlines ballooning.

Modern food processing goes back at least as far as World War II, but I'm especially interested in the changes that have taken place during my lifetime. Lots of popular processed foods came into being while I was a kid: Tab, Diet Coke, Pringles, Gatorade, Slurpees, and Pop-Tarts are all children of the 1960s, like me. But what I most remember from my childhood is the breakfast cereal.

Cold breakfast cereals have been around ever since the Kellogg brothers invented Corn Flakes in the 1890s, but it was only in the 1960s and '70s that the category really began to hit its stride, surging toward the $10 billion business it is today. More and more women were working outside the home, which put new pressure on the breakfast hour as mom raced around trying to get her family, and herself, clothed, fed, and out the door in time for work and school. Mothers needed something to feed their children that would be faster and easier to prepare than old standbys like cooked porridges or bacon and eggs.

The cold cereals that Kellogg's, Post, and General Mills were turning out by the truckload seemed like the perfect answer. They appeared wholesome enough, especially at a time when animal fats were starting to be viewed as health risks. Kids could pour their own cereal and milk with minimal intervention from mom and dad. And the best part? Kids loved them. There would be no arguments at the breakfast table. By the 1950s, new technology gave manufacturers the ability to sugar-coat their cereals, delivering a huge burst of sweetness with every bite. As we now know, children are all but powerless to resist the lure of sugar, even in quantities that would taste overbearing to an adult. By the time I was born in 1959, many cereals were a staggering 50 percent sugar or more by weight.

When I was a really little kid, my mom fed us Cheerios (this was back when Cheerios came in one variety and were relatively nutritious). I recall being happy enough with that breakfast. Then the advertisements came along. On Saturday

> About 70 percent of the calories we eat today come from highly processed foods, foods that didn't even exist before the twentieth century.

mornings, in between Looney Tunes and Tom and Jerry, a whole new set of characters beamed into my living room through the magic of our brand-new color TV. There was Tony the Tiger, Sonny the Cuckoo Bird, and Lucky the Leprechaun, all much more persuasive at selling the merits of Frosted Flakes, Cocoa Puffs, and Lucky Charms to a five-year-old than my mom could be with her Cheerios. My favorite was Cap'n Crunch, the goofy cartoon pirate. I couldn't wait to get my hands on that cereal, and would beg and plead for it at the grocery store.

There was just one problem: I might as well have been eating candy bars for breakfast. Cereals like Cap'n Crunch were made primarily from sugar, and what else they contained had little nutritive value. Then and now, the harsh refining, extruding, steaming, drying, and toasting used to produce breakfast cereals removes almost any of the natural nutrients found in grains.

Then there's the matter of fortification. Breakfast cereals, like most other highly processed grains, are dosed up with added vitamins in a half-hearted effort to replace the nutrients lost in processing. But as scientists now understand, the brute addition of a handful of vitamins and minerals does not replace the complex web of nutri-

ents, polyphenols, flavanols, carotenoids, and the like delivered by whole foods. Fortification is basically an admission on the part of manufacturers that they know this stuff isn't good for you.

Cereal wasn't the only processed food invading the breakfast table during my childhood in the early '60s. Tang, that lab-made concoction composed of sugar, preservatives, texturing agents, and artificial flavorings—plus ascorbic acid, for vitamin C!—had begun to replace real orange juice. Though it was released in 1958, it really picked up steam after 1962, when the astronaut John Glenn returned from space and proclaimed Tang to be the best thing about his time up there. You couldn't dream up a better endorsement. Boring old OJ didn't stand a chance against a drink engineered by scientists and adored by an astronaut.

So there we were, eating our Cap'n Crunch and drinking our Tang and generally believing that if a big, blue-chip company sold it to us with the government's say-so, it must be safe to eat. We were incredibly trusting in those days. What I've learned since about the inner workings of the federal regulatory system has awoken me to two facts: it is entirely beholden to the big money of the food industry, and even when they're trying to get things right, they almost

> Unconstrained by any true oversight, the food industry today is free to dump additives into our food virtually unregulated.

*The same strategy used by Gatorade to "disparage" water!*

always get them wrong.

The Food and Drug Administration, or FDA, is responsible for ensuring the safety of all edibles aside from meat, poultry, and eggs, which are handled by the USDA (U.S. Department of Agriculture). But most people drastically overestimate the extent of the FDA's efforts in overseeing food additives, imagining that—as with drugs—extensive testing, debate, and review take place before a new chemical ends up in your dinner. Well, dream on.

The FDA has had formal authority over food additives since 1958, when the Food Additive Amendment began requiring manufacturers to prove the safety of any new additive brought to market. It's easy to see the conflict of interest inherent in having an additive manufacturer sponsor its own testing; of course, this should fall to a neutral third party with no financial stake in the results.

But the real problem is far worse, and lies with something called the "GRAS" list, a massive loophole in the law that has led to very, very few of the additives on the market today having undergone any kind of formal review and approval process. As part of the 1958 law, Congress established a repository for food additives Generally Recognized as Safe, or GRAS, such as spices, vinegar, and yeast—items that had long been in the food supply and were not suspected to be harmful. For these items and ones like them, companies could bypass the lengthy FDA approval process and simply petition for the substance to be added to the GRAS list by demonstrating that there was a "consensus among scientific experts" that the ingredient was safe. In practice, this usually meant a food manufacturer convening a panel of its own experts to vouch for the ingredient.

Spotting an easy way to circumvent a tedious and expensive approval process, food manufacturers have submitted chemicals for GRAS status that were never intended to pass without more stringent investigation—and the "consensus among scientific experts" has proven a flimsy standard. The Center for Public Integrity found that at least four of the top ten GRAS panel experts had also served as scientific consultants for cigarette makers. The top ten most frequently hired panelists have each sat on two dozen or more panels, essentially proving that these boards are staffed with "yes-men" just looking for a payout.

It was in 1997 when the FDA's oversight really took a nosedive. As the rate of innovation in food additives quickened, reviewing GRAS petitions started to overwhelm the understaffed agency. So, the FDA decided to change the GRAS process.

Fortification is basically an admission on the part of manufacturers that they know this stuff isn't good for you.

Instead of petitioning for GRAS status, chemical companies and food manufacturers would simply decide for themselves about the safety of the additives they invented. Even notifying the agency of the newfangled substance would be purely voluntary. Today, virtually anything added to your food can be claimed as GRAS, completely circumventing the government's role in assessing its safety.

According to the *Washington Post*, only two petitions for formal approval of new additives are filed annually, on average, by food and chemical companies. The agency receives dozens of GRAS notifications. Hundreds of other food chemicals and ingredients have been introduced without any FDA notification whatsoever.

As FDA oversight has withered, new preservatives, emulsifiers, colorings, flavorings, thickeners, and the like are flooding the market at a record pace. Today, the Pew Charitable Trusts estimates the number of additives in our food at around 10,000; the FDA's database contains only 3,000. By comparison, shortly after the 1958 law was passed, that number was around 800. Less than half of the food additives on the market have been the subject of any published human or animal studies.

Then there is the matter of chemical interactions. Due to the nature of our modern food supply, it's not unusual for a consumer to eat over a hundred different chemicals in a single day. Even if each had been thoroughly tested, it would be impossible to evaluate the infinite ways in which chemicals and nutrients combine and interact with each other, and what impact those interactions have on human health.

And if the FDA isn't sure which additives now show up in our food supply, and in what combinations, they have even less information about the quantities in which they appear. Food companies are not required to disclose—to the FDA or on their packaging—quantities of each ingredient used, so it's anybody's guess how much autolyzed yeast extract, say, or sodium benzoate the average American is consuming on a daily basis. We could be chowing down on these chemicals in far larger volumes than was ever anticipated. Caffeine is a good example. When it was certified for use in foods in 1959, no one ever anticipated the invention of the "energy" drink, which contains that chemical in large enough quantities to sicken or kill people. Dosage, and context within the rest of our food intake, is everything. Any substance, no matter how mild—even water—in large enough doses becomes toxic.

Even the FDA itself realizes that the chemical stew that lurks inside our food supply has

> Due to the nature of our modern food supply, it's not unusual for a consumer to eat over a hundred different chemicals in a single day.

gotten beyond them. "We simply do not have the information to vouch for the safety of many of these chemicals," Michael Taylor, the FDA's deputy commissioner for food, told the *Washington Post*.

So, unconstrained by any true oversight, the food industry today is free to dump additives into our food virtually unregulated. I don't believe that large food companies are all evil or "out to get us," but I do think they are rational. They respond only to threats to their profitability, or demonstrable, traceable short-term health issues (such as food poisoning outbreaks) stemming from their products. They do not concern themselves with the long-term health implications of the food they sell.

Fabricating food from industrial additives allows food companies to both lower their costs and increase our consumption by engineering textures, flavors, and shapes designed to be impossible to resist. Food companies make cheap, addictive food on purpose—because consumers buy it. We cannot expect them to make responsible health choices when doing so goes against their own self-interest; we can only encourage them to do so by demanding better products and forcing more transparent disclosure of what's in them. Then, we can vote with our wallets; our greatest power over food

> After a long century of loading up on artificial additives, Americans are finally beating a path back to a more natural way of eating. But this is just the beginning.

companies and our general health is where we spend our next dollar.

The good news is, after years of soaring additive usage, we are finally seeing flashes of hope. People like you and me have awoken to the potential dangers of food additives, and are demanding change from the companies that use them. Seeing a threat to their profitability, large food companies have begun to respond, addressing consumers' concerns about the chemicals that fill their foods. As I write this, Panera, the quick-service restaurant, has recently announced that it will remove at least 150 artificial additives from its products. The industrial chicken grower Tyson Foods says it has plans to eliminate human antibiotics from its chicken production, and Chick-fil-A and McDonald's have committed to providing customers with antibiotic-free poultry within the next two to five years. Kraft is removing artificial colors and preservatives from its macaroni and cheese and will replace them with natural spices. Kellogg's is launching a line of cereals without preservatives or artificial colors and flavors. Pepsi will no longer use aspartame as an artificial sweetener in its diet sodas. This is progress. After a long century of loading up on artificial additives, Americans are finally beating a path back to a more natural way of eating. But this is just the beginning.

Pure Food Nation:
A Call to Action

IN THE PRECEDING CHAPTERS, I'VE GIVEN YOU ALL MY BEST AMMUNITION FOR WHY YOU SHOULD ADOPT A PURE DIET, RIDDING YOURSELF OF THE HARMFUL ADDITIVES THAT LURK IN SO MUCH OF OUR FOOD.

I've encouraged you to take your health into your own hands, listening to your body and its needs rather than following the nutritional guidance offered by the government and food manufacturers—who, time after time, tend to get it wrong.

But the fact is, without the support of these major institutions, we can only do so much to improve the way we eat. Our diets can only be as pure as the food, and information about that food, that's made available to us. That's where the government and "Big Food" come in.

Beyond the choices we each make in our own diets day-to-day, here are the changes that I'd like to see implemented by lawmakers and food executives:

➤ Improve transparency by requiring both food manufacturers and restaurants to list all ingredients in all the food and beverages they sell, including liquor, beer, and wine.

➤ Implement a ban on the advertising, and all marketing, of food and beverages to youth.

➤ Empower schools to model healthy eating through a ban on the sale of junk food and sugary drinks, the construction of full-functioning kitchens, and the reintroduction of home economics classes to teach food literacy and cooking skills.

While we wait for these major changes to take place, you can take three immediate steps to help reshape how food companies advertise to kids, and how kids learn about and consume food and beverages:

➤ Vote for legislators who prioritize a pure food agenda and keep them accountable. The scorecards at FoodPolicyAction.org are a great resource to help you find the lawmakers who are voting to enact responsible food policy legislation.

➤ Vote with your dollars. Buy the purest products that you can afford, produced by companies that prioritize ingredient transparency. Support local farmers' markets and build relationships with the growers, butchers, and dairies in your region.

➤ Join the conversation at www.purefoodrevolution.org.

# The Pure Food Way

# A PURE FOOD MANIFESTO

## WHAT DOES IT MEAN TO EAT PURE?

Most of us feel that our lives are too hectic these days. Dual-income households abound. Smartphones bring our offices into our living rooms and onto our kitchen tables. It's a challenge juggling family, career, and household responsibilities, before we even get around to thinking about personal health. That's why I've grown frustrated with the complicated and contradictory nutritional guidance offered by diet gurus and the federal government; not only does the advice change every few years, but it also makes eating healthy seem hopelessly complicated. Personally, I've never been a dieter, but I've watched plenty of friends and family struggle with different schemes aimed at making them healthier, thinner, more energetic—whatever. Whether you're following the Paleo diet, Weight Watchers, or even just eating according to the USDA's food pyramid, choosing meals can feel like a problem-solving exercise. Was that side of spinach one serving of vegetables or two? How many calories were in my breakfast muffin? If I skip dessert tonight, can I have pancakes for breakfast tomorrow? It's enough to make your head spin.

In my experience, if you commit yourself to the simple goal of avoiding additives, the rest falls into place. Counting calories, fat grams, or carbs, eliminating gluten, dialing down your meat consumption, and trying

to remove all the sugar from your life are unnecessary measures. By cutting out additives, which are almost universally found in industrially produced food, you will automatically eat more of the "good stuff": whole grains, vegetables, fruits, and high-quality animal products.

New science is constantly emerging that addresses the impact of various food additives on our health, and good research is critical to improving experts' understanding of the safety of the food we eat. But you'll notice that I rarely reference studies throughout this book. Why? Many of the studies out there today are funded by the food manufacturers themselves, commissioned with a particular, advantageous outcome in mind. For every thorough third-party evaluation of a given food additive, there are several more undertaken by research groups whose objectivity is in question due to funding ties to the processed food industry.

Even the well-designed, independently funded studies are of limited use when trying to navigate the chemical stew that is our modern food supply. That's because none of them study, or ever could hope to study, food additives in the context in which we encounter them: combined in infinite arrangements and dosage levels, and ingested over the course of decades. Because I don't believe that adequate science exists to really evaluate the impact of food additives on our bodies, my personal decision has been to

*No one even talks about this and it is huge!*

forget the individual studies and simply avoid food additives wholesale. Given that there are over 10,000 additives in our food supply today, with more always being invented and renamed, you could go crazy trying to keep track of them all.

## WHAT COUNTS AS A FOOD ADDITIVE?

So if we're trying to avoid additives, what are they in the first place? Anything added to a whole food during processing counts as an additive. I'm primarily concerned with substances on the ingredient label that sound like they came from a chemicals catalog (potassium bromate, autolyzed yeast extract, sodium benzoate) rather than the ones that you'd find in a home kitchen (salt, water, spices, vinegar, lemon juice).

You'll notice that I say to avoid food additives, not avoid "processed" food. That's because nearly all foods, unless you're bringing whole hogs into your kitchen or picking wheat berries off the stalk, are processed in some way. My concern is with foods that have been heavily manipulated, which almost always involves the use of multiple food additives.

Additives fulfill many different functions to change the way a food tastes, smells, looks, and feels, how much it costs to produce, and how long it lasts on the shelf. There are thickeners, gelling agents, and foaming agents to produce and maintain certain textures. Anticaking agents keep powders, like spice mixes, from clumping. Antioxidants stop fats from going rancid. Preservatives prevent spoilage. Raising agents help bread rise and bulking agents function as low-calorie fillers. Colorings make foods more attractive and flavor enhancers either augment, or completely replace, the flavors naturally found in food. Emulsifiers and firming agents keep foods from separating. Glazing agents coat their surfaces, as with the wax on fruit that improves its appearance. Humectants prevent foods from drying out. Fats, salt, and sugars are all used to make foods tastier and more addictive, drawing eaters to consume them in larger quantities than was once thought possible. Even whole foods have their own categories of additives, such as the pesticides and petroleum-based fertilizers used when growing fruits and vegetables, and antibiotics and hormones fed to animals.

## WHY EAT PURE?

For me, eating pure started in response to a food allergy: MSG gave me headaches, so I took it out of my life. Over the course of thirty years of gradually eliminating additives from my life, I've noticed that when I eat pure I have more energy, sleep better, carry less body fat, and maybe partly as a result of all those things, have a more positive outlook on life.

Beyond all the day-to-day mental and physical benefits, the best reason to avoid food additives is because we don't know what long-term impact they will have on our bodies—and neither does the FDA. Michael Taylor, the FDA's deputy commissioner for food, has gone on the record admitting as much (see "A Short History of Processed Food" for more details). So, consuming the thousands of additives floating around our food supply is playing Russian roulette with your health. Surely all of the additives aren't dangerous, but we can't yet say with confidence which ones are.

## WHO SHOULD EAT PURE?

Anyone can benefit from removing additives from his or her diet, but taking steps to eliminate them is particularly important for children, whose rapidly developing bodies and brains are especially sensitive to chemicals. Ironically, food marketed toward kids and their parents is some of the most additive-laden junk on the market, so it takes a lot of vigilance and label reading to avoid them.

People with chronic illnesses such as heart disease or diabetes—and even asthma or allergies—would also benefit disproportionately from a diet free from food additives, some of which have been shown to cause these ailments.

# PUTTING IT INTO PRACTICE: HOW TO EAT PURE

## THE COMMITMENT

Like anything else in life, you can't get the benefits of eating pure without a little bit of work. Here are four changes you should anticipate making in order to really transform the way you eat:

➤ Plan ahead: The most heavily adulterated foods tend to be convenience foods: frozen meals, fast food, energy bars, instant soups, and the like. These are the things you turn to when it's mealtime and you're without a game plan. It's much harder to make healthy decisions when you're tired and hungry, and that's why it's important to plan your meals ahead of time. Pick a quiet time of the week— like Sunday mornings—when you can sit down and map out seven days of breakfasts, lunches, and dinners for all the members of your household, plus do an inventory of your healthy snack options to make sure you have enough on hand. Spending the extra time up-front will help you maximize leftovers, minimize trips to the grocery store, and stretch a single recipe across several different dinners. For example, Old Bay Roasted Turkey Breast (page 138) can be served with sides for dinner, then leftovers can be used in sandwiches, Turkey Tortilla Soup (page 144), and Turkey Burritos Ahogados (page 141). The best way to motivate yourself to cook from scratch is to already have the ingredients, and recipes, on hand.

➤ Spend more at the grocery store: It is generally true that high-quality, unadulterated foods cost more than ones loaded with industrial fillers. That's because they simply cost more to make, whether you are growing a calf to adulthood without hormones or baking bread free from dough conditioners and preservatives. So, you should expect your grocery bill to climb a little higher once you start weaning yourself off highly processed food. Some of the extra grocery expense will be counteracted by eating out at restaurants less; since it's exceedingly hard to know what additives are in restaurant meals, it's best to dine out only on special occasions. But, you may still find that your total food budget rises once you start eating high-quality whole foods. For many people, this will mean trading entertainment or clothing for a healthier way of eating. Although it may be a hard adjustment at first, think of it this way: Americans at one time spent a much higher share of their budgets on food. According to the USDA's Economic Research Service, between 1960 and 2007, the share of disposable personal income spent on food fell from 17.5 to 9.6 percent. Over the same period, however, the percent of America's Gross Domestic Product spent on health care rose from 5 percent to 17.4 percent. As the old saying goes, "You can either pay your doctor or pay your grocer." I'd rather pay my grocer.

➤ Prepare for waste: Eating pure means basing your diet around highly perishable ingredients like fresh meats and fish, vegetables, and fruits, avoiding many of the foods best equipped to sit on a shelf for eons. Inevitably, if your fridge is properly stocked with the makings for healthful meals and snacks to meet your daily needs, some of it will go bad and need to be discarded. I know people really fear and loathe wasting food,

but it's important to understand that some waste is inevitable, and it's a good sign that you are shopping and cooking correctly. If you aim only to have exactly as much fresh food as you will use without waste, you will end up running short and seeking out more processed forms of food.

*If it doesn't go bad then it's not good*

➤ Devote more time to cooking: The best way to know for sure that your food is pure is to make it with your own two hands, which is why I decided to write this cookbook. Even if you're smart about planning meals in advance and making the most of your time in the kitchen, cooking is likely to be a bigger part of your life once you're focused on eating pure. You may be surprised to find that that's actually a good thing! I've discovered over the years that cooking can be creative, relaxing, and very satisfying.

## MAKING COMPROMISES

Before I delve into the specific information that will help you launch your pure food lifestyle, a word of advice: don't let perfect be the enemy of good. Eating pure is a lifestyle, not a short-term diet, which means that making realistic and manageable choices from day to day is going to lead to greater success in the long run than being an absolute stickler for only zero additive foods. That means if you're in the middle of a road trip and eating from a gas station convenience store, don't have a meltdown. Choose the potato chips (three ingredients) not the Flamin' Hot Cheetos (almost thirty ingredients). If you absolutely love Oreo cookies, try to eat them once a

month, not once a week. I've been at this for almost thirty years, and I still find myself in situations—when I travel, go out to eat with colleagues or friends, or my boys simply demand certain foods that don't fit the pure food mantra—where I wind up eating things that I know aren't so good for me. I don't sweat these situations, because I don't expect myself to bat 1000. The fact of the matter is that additives are everywhere you look. Strive to make better choices, not perfect ones.

## UNDERSTANDING ORGANIC

Most of the health claims written on food labels are meaningless (or even a good sign that the food isn't good for you—see "On Meaningless Marketing Claims" following), but the Certified Organic seal carries some real weight to it. Foods marketed as Certified Organic must fulfill a specific set of requirements, and compliance is strictly enforced by the USDA. By definition, Certified Organic products must be made without the use of chemical pesticides, synthetic fertilizers, and genetically modified organisms (GMOs). There's a specific set of guidelines that apply just for meats, poultry, and dairy products, which I explain in more detail in the following chapter. A product must be 95 percent or more organic to carry the Certified Organic seal.

Looking for the Certified Organic seal is especially useful when buying fruits and vegetables. In these cases, pesticides and synthetic fertilizers are the primary additives you should be concerned about, and you can feel confident that organic versions are clean.

When it comes to packaged goods, however, Certified Organic status doesn't mean that a product is additive-free. Lots of organic packaged goods—granola bars, cereals, salad dressings, frozen meals—count as what I call "organic junk," loaded with added fats, sugars, salt, and plenty of other additives, and yet still labeled organic. For instance, Vermont Bread Company's Organic Multigrain bread includes all of the following: cane sugar, added wheat gluten, molasses, soybean oil, enzymes, cultured wheat starch, citric acid, reduced-fat soy flour, ascorbic acid, and soy lecithin. Many of those additives are classified as "organic," but that doesn't make them good for you (and real, fresh bread doesn't require any of them).

It's also important to understand that a product doesn't need to be Certified Organic to be high quality and chemical-free. Undergoing the official USDA certification process is expensive and time-consuming, and often out of reach for small farmers whose practices are as good as or better than what's required to qualify them for the label. The milk we use for Beecher's Handmade Cheese isn't Certified Organic, for instance; we have individual relationships with all of our dairies and understand their farming practices in depth, so it's not necessary for us to rely on government certifications.

Very little meat has Certified Organic status. It's simply too difficult and expensive, especially in the case of free-ranging animals, to provide them with 100 percent organic feed.

If you are shopping at a farmers' market, whether for meats or fruits or vegetables, don't bother looking for Certified Organic products, as you won't be likely to find many. Simply talk to the farmers about their operations, and ask them about their use of pesticides, fertilizer, antibiotics, and hormones.

## STAYING "UNDER FIVE"

In the interest of keeping things simple, a good rule for buying packaged goods (and one that we teach in our Pure Food Kids workshops) is to stick to foods with under five ingredients on the label. Five isn't a magic number—it's fairly arbitrary, in fact—but the fewer additives used, the less adulterated a food tends to be.

## ABOUT GMOS

GMOs—or genetically modified organisms—are living things whose genes have been deliberately altered in a laboratory to endow the organism with a desirable trait. This might mean a wheat strain that produces its own insecticide, or a soybean plant that's resistant to viruses. Today, most of the genetically modified plants out there are field crops like corn, rice, soybeans, sugar beets, and wheat, which are used heavily in packaged goods, as well as in animal feed.

My beef with GMO plants is that they create unstable, Frankenstein-esque combinations of plant, animal, bacteria, and virus genes, and their long-term impacts on the environment and human health are not easy to predict. The European Union, Japan, and Australia, among other countries, are skeptical enough of GMOs to have strict laws (and in some cases, outright bans) governing their production and sale.

In the U.S., however, regulations are much more lax—companies aren't even required to declare their use of GMO ingredients on labels. There is, however, one way to know that you're eating GMO-free food: buy items that bear the Certified Organic seal. By law, Certified Organic foods must be free of GMOs.

## ON MEANINGLESS MARKETING CLAIMS

*"Contains Real Fruit!"*
*"A Good Source of Fiber!"*
*"Heart Healthy!"*
Packaged foods today tend to be covered with phrases like these, touting their various health benefits. These statements are almost without exception meaningless. My general rule of thumb is that the more health claims a product has on its label, the less healthy it's likely to be. These are usually highly processed foods with big marketing budgets employed to trick you into thinking they're healthy.

Another common marketing tactic revolves around names and logos, and what they imply about the company. Countless brands today look to cultivate a healthy, natural image by choosing names intended to evoke small, local, back-to-the-earth–style operations. Look around the supermarkets and you'll see Cascadian Farm (owned by General Mills), Stonyfield Farm (a subsidiary of the multinational conglomerate Groupe Danone), and Creekstone Farms (owned by the investment group Sun Capital Partners). A name that makes consumers think of rolling farmland and small-batch production rather than enormous manufacturing plants costs nothing, and buys consumer trust. Don't let yourself

*Good rule of thumb*

fall into this trap. Even if there once was a "farm" involved, it's no longer relevant to the industrial product except as a marketing image to convince you that it's "healthy."

To help you sort through fact and fiction, I've compiled a list of some of the most common meaningless marketing claims to watch out for:

➤ "Multigrain" or "Made with whole grain": The only way to know that a product is truly whole grain—that is, it includes the germ, bran, and endosperm of the grain—is to look for the phrase "100 percent whole grain." Multigrain simply means that there are multiple grains used, some or all of which may be refined; a food can tout that it's "made with whole grains" if it contains any amount of whole grain, no matter how small.

➤ "Natural": Meat, poultry, and eggs labeled "natural" must be minimally processed and contain no artificial ingredients—but the term provides no information about farm practices, such as the use of antibiotics or hormones. That's right: "natural" meat can still be treated with antibiotics and hormones! There are currently no standards or legal requirements for the use of the marketing claim "natural" on other types of food, making it utterly meaningless.

➤ "No MSG": Believe it or not, products labeled "No MSG" or "No added MSG" sometimes do, in fact, contain free glutamates—which are one and the same as MSG. Free glutamates go by so many different names aside from MSG—autolyzed yeast, hydrolyzed vegetable protein, soy protein concentrate, and natural flavoring are just a few—that food producers can include these substances while advertising the item as "MSG-free." While the FDA has recognized the issue and technically prohibits any products containing free glutamates from being labeled as MSG-free, the rule is not universally enforced.

➤ "No trans fat": Trans fats are now universally recognized as the most harmful type of fat in our food supply. While public interest groups are working toward an all-out FDA ban on the ingredient, they are still lurking in small quantities in plenty of products. What's worse: products can boast "No Trans Fat!" and list 0 grams trans fat on their nutrition labels as long as they contain less than 0.5 gram of trans fat per serving. That might not sound like a lot, but for foods with unrealistically small serving sizes, those fractional grams of trans fats add up fast. To tell whether a food really contains trans fat, look for the word "hydrogenated" in the ingredients list.

➤ "No nitrates/nitrites added": This claim simply means that no synthetic nitrates and nitrites have been added as preservatives to items such as deli meats and hot dogs, but the producer can still use natural nitrates and nitrites, which are just as harmful.

➤ "Cage-free": This one isn't directly related to additives, but a good thing to look out for

on food labels, especially if you care about animal welfare (as we all should). You'll often see this label on egg cartons to imply that the laying hens lived a good life. The claim does guarantee that the chickens weren't caged, but they can still be overcrowded into dark, fetid barns, which isn't much better.

➤ "Free-range": Similarly to "cage-free," "free-range" isn't an additive-related issue, but I wanted to clarify its meaning nonetheless since it's often misunderstood. Producers using the free-range label must demonstrate to the USDA that their animals have been allowed "access to the outside"—but there are no requirements for the quality or size of the outdoor space. So don't assume rolling, green hills are involved.

## ON THE WORST OF THE WORST

I've already told you that the food supply contains so many different additives, with new ones being added all the time, that I find it to be a losing battle trying to keep up with them all. Mostly, I just strive to avoid additives of all kinds in my diet. However, there are a few that I consider to be so toxic that I really go out of my way to avoid them whenever possible.

➤ Artificial dyes: Several petroleum-based artificial dyes used in the likes of sugary drinks, candies, ice pops, meats, and many other grocery products have been linked to hyperactivity and ADHD in children. The European Union and the British government have already taken steps to end the use

of these dyes, but they are still recognized as safe by the FDA.

➤ Artificial sweeteners: Although many people think of artificially sweetened foods, such as low-cal yogurts and diet sodas, as "healthy" alternatives to sugary versions, this simply is not the case. At a minimum, they mess with your body's natural ability to use a food's sweetness to gauge calorie intake; aspartame, which is marketed under the brands Equal and NutraSweet, has also been linked to an increased risk of cancer in some studies. There's no such thing as a "natural" artificial sweetener, whatever marketers may tell you about their origins.

➤ Azodicarbonamide: This dough "improver" is used to strengthen dough used for bread and rolls (it is also, by the way, used in the production of foamed plastics like yoga mats and shoe soles). It's been linked to asthma and allergic reactions, and when baked, produces chemicals that may be carcinogens.

➤ BHA and BHT: Butylated hydroxyanisole (BHA) and butylated hydroxytoluene (BHT) are preservatives commonly found in cereal, chewing gum, potato chips, fast food, snack foods—you name it. They keep fats from going rancid and preserve the color, smell, and flavor of foods. BHA is considered safe by the FDA, but the National Toxicology Program considers it to be "reasonably anticipated" to be a carcinogen. Evidence that BHT has cancer-causing properties is limited, but its structural similarities to BHA make it suspect.

➤ MSG: If you're like me and have an allergic reaction to MSG—headaches, dizziness, nausea—eating it is a no-go.

➤ Potassium bromate: This dough strengthener, found in baked goods, has been banned in countries around the world because studies have shown that it causes cancer in animals. In the United States, it remains legal.

➤ Propyl gallate: Like BHA and BHT, this chemical keeps fat from spoiling, but some studies have shown it to be a carcinogen and an endocrine disruptor.

➤ Sodium nitrate and sodium nitrite: These preservatives are responsible for the signature taste, long shelf life, and rosy pink color of cured meats like hot dogs and cold cuts. They have long been known to cause gastric cancers. Although they are now used in much smaller quantities than in the past, and some measures have been taken to decrease their toxicity, it's still worth avoiding them.

➤ Trans fats: Trans fat, which is most commonly found in margarine, some fried foods, and crackers, is now known to be the most dangerous type of fat out there. It is a major culprit for heart disease. Trans fats are listed on ingredient labels as "hydrogenated" oils; be sure to avoid them.

## THE BIGGEST LIARS

We all know by now to avoid old-fashioned junk foods like sodas, sugary cereals, and frozen pizzas. But most people aren't aware just how many additives lurk in foods marketed as healthy, from sports drinks to energy bars to low-fat yogurts. These are the products that really get under my skin, because they play on our desires to eat healthy food but deliver exactly the opposite. Coca-Cola may not be good for you, but at least what you see is what you get.

When you're shopping for any type of packaged food, I strongly urge you to read the ingredient list before buying it. If sugar or refined grains are near the top, it's almost definitely not as healthy for you as advertised.

Here's a short list of common, healthy-sounding foods that are wolves in sheep's clothing:

➤ Gluten-free items: Gluten intolerance was once a problem that few people even thought about, but the past several years have seen a surge of interest in avoiding wheat gluten, which some people blame for digestive upset, weight gain, and fatigue. For this reason, items marked "gluten-free" have an aura of health about them. I don't personally buy into the harmful nature of gluten, and believe that it's all the other junk lurking in our foods that's making us feel so sick. But even if you are a gluten avoider, it's important to keep in mind that gluten-free products promise nothing more than the absence of the naturally occurring protein gluten. They are not necessarily otherwise healthy or additive-free.

➤ Special K: I pick on Special K in particular as a breakfast cereal that has branded itself as an effective diet food. In fact, it's made from refined grains, and added sugar is one of its top ingredients. None of these things is known for being especially conducive to weight loss. But for years, Special K's marketers promised that replacing two meals a day with a small bowl of the cereal was a wonderful diet, as if Special K had some sort of magical capacity as a weight loss aid; I think you'd find that replacing two meals a day with any 120-calorie snack would make you lose weight.

➤ Subway sandwich chain: Subway has done a masterful job of marketing itself as "fresh" and "healthy" compared to fast food chains like McDonald's and Burger King. It's anything but. Subway makes a big deal of baking its bread "fresh" and "in-house." While the breads are technically baked in stores, the dough is produced industrially and loaded with literally dozens of additives (up until recently this included azodicarbonamide, which as I've mentioned is a chemical used in making yoga mats). The sandwich fillings are just as bad, with deli meats and dressings containing the usual slew of preservatives, sugar, emulsifiers, nitrites, et cetera. While some of Subway's sandwich options may be low in fat and calories, if you're looking for pure food, this sandwich chain is far from being a good solution.

➤ Vitaminwater and sports drinks: Consumers view sports drinks as performance enhancers fit for high-functioning athletes. In fact, they're basically just a stew of sugar, artificial flavors, and colorants, with no redeeming value unless you're working

out for long periods at high intensity and are in serious need of a blood sugar boost. Vitaminwater is one of the biggest hoaxes out there—it's also packed with sugar (sugar is the second ingredient listed, after water). As for the vitamins it contains, supplementing your diet with isolated vitamins in this way is entirely unnecessary (and ineffective) for most people eating a balanced diet. Gatorade, back when it was even less sugary than it is now, was originally designed to fuel the University of Florida Gators football team, doing two practices a day in the August heat in Florida. As much as the food marketers want you to believe it, your six-year-old tee-baller definitely doesn't need to be drinking this stuff.

➤ Yogurt: Yogurt sales have been on a tear lately, due to its growing reputation as a healthy, low-carb snack. It's true that many yogurts contain live cultures, which are beneficial to digestive health. But the yogurt aisle is also a hornet's nest of added sugars, artificial sweeteners, and colorants, as well as thickeners such as starch and gelatin to increase the body of low-fat products. Sugar is often the second ingredient in yogurts; one little container of Yoplait strawberry yogurt contains 18 grams of sugar, the equivalent of more than four sugar cubes. While some fruit-flavored yogurts contain actual fruit, many get by with fruit juice concentrates and added color. If you're buying yogurt, always buy plain (ideally organic) versions and sweeten it yourself at home. And always, always read the label before you buy. Pure yogurt doesn't need to contain anything more than milk or cream and live cultures.

# Pantry + Tools

# PURE PANTRY REHAB

The first step to cleaning up your diet is cleaning out your pantry.

Throw out anything that you've had on hand for more than six months, or that you can't remember buying to begin with. Even though pantry items are often referred to as "nonperishable," the better term is "less perishable." All ingredients degrade over time, so even durable items like grains, vinegars, and jarred sauces shouldn't hang out in your cabinets indefinitely. If they're pure foods, they are likely to be stale (whole grains, crackers), rancid (nuts, oils), or their flavors greatly diminished (spices, teas).

Now, go through the items that remain one by one and read the ingredient labels. If they contain additives that are unacceptable to you, toss them. Just how strict you are with this step is a matter of personal preference. Whether you're a "zero tolerance" type who wants to go completely additive-free, or you just want to eliminate the most noxious chemical combos, the important thing is to have in your pantry only foods you'll feel good about eating today, tomorrow, or next week.

Now it's time to begin rebuilding your pantry with pure, nourishing foods.

Avoid "stocking up," or buying items without an immediate use in mind because you will maybe, possibly need them in a recipe someday. In my experience, these items invariably end up sitting around and gathering dust until they're too old to use. What a waste.

Try to keep only as much in your pantry as you can see when you open the cupboard doors, without rearranging or removing items. I've found that out of sight is out of mind, and foods that I have to dig for end up sitting unused. Since eating pure means living mostly on fresh, whole foods and making your own sauces and condiments whenever possible, there shouldn't be too much competition for space in your pantry, anyway.

## FOCUS ON WHOLE FOODS

The majority of your diet—and by extension, your pantry—should be made up of whole foods: fruits, vegetables, intact grains, fish, meat, and dairy. Whole foods are single-ingredient items that you could easily picture in nature.

It seems like choosing between whole foods should be very straightforward from an additives perspective—after all, what could possibly be in a head of broccoli besides broccoli?—but in fact, these are some of the trickiest foods to shop for. Unlike packaged goods, fruits, vegetables, meats, and fish are not required to list the additives that might have been used in the course of growing and processing them, like antibiotics, hormones, steroids, pesticides, and numerous processing aids. So, prawns or scallops might be soaked in sodium tripolyphosphate solution after they're caught, and there is no legal requirement to disclose that. Meats might be flushed with carbon monoxide gas before packaging to maintain their pink color and to prevent spoilage. Apples can be coated in food-grade wax to protect them, and make them more shiny and appealing. Unfortunately, none of these things needs to be disclosed on the label.

For this reason, the absolute best way to buy whole foods is to know enough about the ranchers, fisherfolk, and farmers who grew your food to understand how it was raised and processed. This involves visiting a lot of farmers' markets, mail-ordering fish and meat direct from the producers, and seeking out independent butcher shops, fishmongers, bakeries, and cheese shops where you are at most one step removed from the people making or catching your food. It's certainly not the most efficient way to shop for groceries, but you're likely to find forging these relationships to be immensely rewarding.

For all the times when shopping this way isn't possible, here's a practical guide to choosing whole foods at the grocery store.

## DAIRY

Since the 1990s, some American dairies have been injecting their cows with a hormone called rBST (recombinant bovine somatotropin), also known as rBGH (recombinant bovine growth hormone), to make them produce more milk; the stress on their bodies caused by such high milk production then necessitates the use of antibiotics to cure (or prevent) nasty udder infections.

When it comes to milk, the best solution is farm-fresh milk that's been minimally processed. Milk in this form has the benefit of being nonhomogenized, which means the fat globules have been left as is, rather than going through a procedure to break them down and disperse them evenly throughout the milk—just another form of processing that isn't really necessary. If you can't find organic or farm-fresh milk, look for cartons labeled "hormone-free."

Yogurts and cottage cheese are often pretty vile stuff masquerading as health food. Cottage cheese, except for a very few products made from artisan cheesemakers, is simply cheese curd floating in a soup of additives. There are some good yogurts out there, but many contain huge quantities of sugar as well as thickeners and artificial flavors (for more details, see "The Biggest Liars," page 42). Reading the ingredient list is a must when it comes to these kinds of dairy products.

When it comes to cheese, artisan varieties, which are made with whole milk in small batches, often by hand and using traditional methods, are the best bet. I hardly need mention that you should avoid processed cheese, which is made from cheese scraps that are heated and treated with a host of additives.

## FRUITS AND VEGETABLES

The best place to buy produce is at a local farmers' market, and that's not just because it's way more fun to shop out in the fresh air instead of under the fluorescent glare of supermarket lights. It's because the fruits and vegetables found at a farmers' market will almost always be the freshest available to you, since they haven't been carted across the country or the world before they end up in your shopping basket. Farmers' markets also give you the opportunity to speak directly to the men and women who grew your food, so that you can get to know their operations and ask questions about their use of chemicals.

I don't mean to make supermarkets sound like a bad option. In fact, grocery stores have improved their produce departments dramatically in the past decade or so, and you're likely to find lots of good options (many of them organic) even in the most basic chain store. Buying from supermarkets is usually more economical, and often more convenient, than relying on farmers' markets; if these factors get you to buy more fresh fruits and vegetables, that's all that matters.

Don't hesitate to use your local store's produce buyer as a resource. These men and women know more than you realize about the origins of the fruits and vegetables on the shelves, and are usually eager to share that information with you.

If you're shopping in a grocery store, choose organic fruits and vegetables whenever possible. This applies in particular to apples, nectarines, peaches, strawberries, grapes, celery, spinach, bell peppers, cucumbers, cherry tomatoes, snap peas, and potatoes, the so-called "dirty dozen" produce items that carry the highest pesticide residues.

Being organic doesn't guarantee that the produce will taste better, be fresher, or be more nutritious, but it does at least tell you that the foods in question were grown from non-GMO seeds, without the use of pesticides, herbicides, and petroleum-based fertilizers.

EYE OF ROUND ROAST, PAGE 94

## MEATS

Just like fresh produce, raw meats aren't required to carry ingredient labels that tell you about which chemicals were used in the course of raising the animals, or processing them for sale at a grocery store.

You should be wary when buying meats, because there's lots of misleading information floating around on those packages, starting with the brand names and logos. As I mentioned in the previous chapter, a meat packager can have a quaint-sounding name—Applegate Farms, Creekstone Farms—and a package displaying beautiful green pasture, and still operate out of a 50,000-square-foot warehouse on the outskirts of some city.

You'll see the term "natural" on a lot of meat

labels, which on its own doesn't tell you much about how an animal was raised or what additives it might have been fed throughout its life (for more information on the legal definition of "natural," see page 39). Buying meat that is labeled as antibiotic- and hormone-free is a good place to start.

And when it comes to buying meats, from ground beef to leg of lamb to chicken, you'll find Certified Organic seals few and far between. As mentioned above, even high-quality, additive-free meats are rarely organic, because of the cost and difficulty of ensuring that an animal's feed is organic. Farmers argue that they aren't able to raise the price of organic meats enough to cover the added costs of producing them, given that most people are happy to pay a small premium for meats labeled "natural."

This is a shame, because Certified Organic standards are by far the most stringent, and the best way to ensure that your meat is additive-free. Certified Organic animals must be fed exclusively Certified Organic feed, cannot be treated with hormones and antibiotics, cannot be fed animal by-products, cannot be routinely confined, must have access to the outdoors and sunlight, and cattle must have access to pasture. Farms are routinely inspected for compliance with all of these standards.

When buying beef, consumers today are much too focused on "grass-fed" as a marker of quality. For one, terms like "grass-fed" and "grass-finished" aren't strictly regulated, so you may not be buying what you think you're buying. But even if a cow is fed exclusively on grass from birth to slaughter, it doesn't make that animal happier, healthier, purer, or certainly tastier than one fed in the correct, humane way on grain.

When it comes to lunchmeats—deli-case ham, turkey, roast beef, and the like—these are some of the most toxic supermarket items out there. They contain heavy doses of sodium nitrite, a preservative that has been proven to be carcinogenic. They also often contain BHA or BHT to keep fats from going rancid, enzymes to soften the meat, binders, thickeners, emulsifiers, corn syrup, MSG, phosphates to pump up their moisture content, and color fixatives to keep the meat looking attractive for far longer than it has any right to. Deli meats are a truly appalling stew of chemicals, and should be avoided entirely.

*Really try to avoid*

## FISH

Of all the foods we buy, fish is perhaps the most difficult to shop for, because of the scant information provided on labels and the tendency for that information to be inaccurate. This is why buying fish from a trustworthy source is especially critical.

The first rule of thumb is to always choose wild fish over farmed. While some well-run, clean fish farms do exist, the majority are the aquatic versions of the putrid feedlots used to fatten cattle in a hurry. Fish are crammed together into small, polluted waters filled with antibiotics, pesticides, chemicals, and waste, and fed pellets made from ground fish, fish oil, and many more unsavory animal and grain products. Especially in the case of salmon, which is probably the most heavily farmed type of fish, this feeding method produces fish much higher in PCBs than wild versions.

PCBs are toxic industrial chemicals (such as agricultural pesticides) that have been banned since the 1970s, but still pollute streams, lakes, and oceans, and accumulate in the fatty tissue of fish. It's impossible to tell how many PCBs are in a given fish unless it's tested—and few are—but farmed fish fed lots of fish meal and fish oils (like many farmed salmon) tend to be among the most heavily contaminated.

Farmed salmon are also fed dyes to turn their flesh that bright, appealing orange/pink of wild versions; based on the feed they eat, their flesh would naturally be a rather unappetizing gray. While the FDA technically requires such use of added colors to be disclosed on the label, this rule is rarely, if ever, obeyed.

Scallops and shrimp/prawns, two of the most popular seafood items in America, are particularly concerning. I recommend avoiding shrimp and prawns entirely, unless you can find a trusted wild source. They are almost without exception farmed in fetid, overcrowded pools, often in Southeast Asia, and treated with sodium tripolyphosphates to pump up their weight before sale. Scallops are also commonly treated with sodium tripolyphosphates, but it's possible to find clean ones if you work with a good distributor (see "Downeast Dayboat," page 162).

And yet, fish mislabeling or outright fraud is so rampant that it's nearly impossible to tell with certainty whether a fish is farmed or wild, what country it came from, or even what species it is. Your best bet is to buy fish only from a high-quality, trusted source—even if

that means eating less fish because what you buy is more expensive.

## GRAINS

Although it's not technically an issue of additives, I use whole grains rather than refined ones whenever possible. Whole grains naturally contain a vast array of vitamins and minerals, and digest more slowly than their refined counterparts. But, they are inconvenient for industrial food companies, because whole grains spoil much more quickly than refined ones, which remain shelf stable for years.

Refined grains—white rice, white flour, cornmeal—are produced by removing the bran and the germ (the sources of all the fiber, vitamins, and minerals) from a grain and retaining just the starchy, sweet endosperm. Since the endosperm on its own is essentially empty calories, many refined grains are then enriched with large quantities of five specific vitamins; the process is intended to make you think that the refined product has all the nutritional benefits of a whole grain, which is far from being true.

Anything that has added vitamins is basically admitting that it isn't good for you

When buying grain-based products, look for products labeled "100% whole grain"—these are the magic words to tell you that the product is truly whole grain. You need to be the most vigilant for wheat, rice, corn, and oat-based products. Quinoa, spelt, amaranth, millet, buckwheat, and barley are all typically only sold in unrefined forms.

With all that in mind, here are the pantry items that I tend to have on hand for cooking at home:

➤ Expeller-pressed safflower oil: This is my go-to oil for cooking. Expeller-pressed grape-seed oil, avocado oil, and peanut oil are also good choices. Why "expeller-pressed"? This means the oil has been squeezed from its source at high pressure, which is a clean way to extract it. Conventional canola and vegetable oils are typically extracted by being bathed in chemical solvents such as hexane, which is a neurotoxin. Not my idea of delicious.

➤ Good olive oil: Olive oil isn't the best fat for cooking—it burns at fairly low temperatures—but I like flavorful, high-quality versions for drizzling on finished dishes and for salad dressings. Store it in a cool, dark place to extend its shelf life.

➤ Granulated garlic and granulated onion: Not to be confused with garlic powder and onion powder, which sometimes contain anti-caking agents to keep them from clumping, granulated garlic and onion are great for use in spice mixes. They also have a more appealing texture than powdered versions, in my opinion.

➤ Salt: I use Morton brand kosher salt and Maldon, a sea salt from England, as a finishing salt.

➤ Vinegars: I keep sherry, white wine, cider, distilled white, and rice vinegars on hand. In the scheme of things, vinegars are some of the longest-lasting food items out there (in fact, they are one of nature's best preservatives). I also use seasoned rice vinegar in a few recipes; some brands contain MSG, so read the label and look for a brand with just sugar and salt added. I'm not a big fan of balsamic vinegar, as I find it too heavy and sweet. If you do use it, though, be sure to get a good one. Authentic balsamic vinegars (always from Modena or Reggio Emilia in Italy) are expensive, but imposters often contain added sugar as well as thickeners and caramel coloring.

➤ Spices, in general: The flavor of spices dulls significantly just days or weeks after they are ground, so rather than buying large spice sets, I recommend buying spices as you use them, and in the smallest quantities possible. Always buy whole spices and grind them to use, if possible. Hold on to ground spices for six months to a year at most.

➤ Flours: Always use unbleached flours, and un-enriched ones if you can find them. I like King Arthur brand, Bob's Red Mill, and Arrowhead Mills. Keep in mind that the shelf life of whole wheat flour is very short—just a few weeks—because the vitamins in the germ portion of the wheat berry go rancid.

➤ Sweeteners: I try to use as little refined sugar (cane sugar, confectioners' sugar, brown sugar) as possible. Maple syrup and honey make good, and more flavorful, natural substitutes.

➤ Mama Lil's Pickled Hot Peppers: I'm crazy for these spicy, sweet, sour jarred peppers. I'm constantly tossing them into pasta, putting them on sandwiches

*find and use these!*

or pureeing them to use as a condiment. The oil that fills the jar is as valuable as the peppers themselves.

➤ Oatmeal: Don't buy "instant" or "quick" oats, which are more processed than whole oats. Oatmeal cooks pretty fast, anyway.

➤ Pasta: I always keep whole wheat or farro pasta on hand; tossed with veggies, it makes an easy lunch or dinner.

➤ Beverages: We drink primarily sparkling or still water in my house, plus tea and the occasional batch of homemade lemonade. Packaged drinks contain so much sugar, whether they're sodas or fruit juices or athletic drinks, that I do my best to steer clear. If you drink coffee, buy whole beans instead of the pre-ground stuff. Not only is the flavor of fresh-ground coffee much better, but also all sorts of cheap fillers (barley, corn, seed husks) can be hidden in ground coffee.

➤ Nuts: Aside from fruits and veggies, nuts are really the only snack food I keep on hand. I buy primarily raw nuts and store them in the freezer to maximize their shelf life.

➤ Carrots: These are really a refrigerator item, not a pantry item, but while we're on the subject of snacks I wanted to mention baby carrots. Contrary to what you might think, these aren't some special breed of sweet, tiny carrot; they're regular carrots that have been shaped and sometimes soaked in sugar water to make them sweeter. Eating a baby carrot is still better than eating a bag of Cheetos, but you're best off eating carrot sticks.

## TOOLS & EQUIPMENT

I don't call for any specialized equipment in this book; the chances are very high that you can make all my recipes with the kitchen tools you already own. But for those of you looking to upgrade your kitchen setup (or outfit one for the first time), here's an account of my essential kitchen toolkit.

As a general note, my motto is: the bigger, the better. I cook in large batches so that I can get the most mileage out of each recipe, and that requires big mixing bowls, skillets, and sheet trays. It never hurts to have a little extra space in your bowl or pan, so when in doubt, buy the bigger size.

A lot of the equipment in my kitchen is made from stainless steel. It's my preferred material because it's durable, nonreactive (that means it doesn't make acidic foods taste strange), and easy to clean, and it distributes heat nicely.

If you only buy three new kitchen tools, I recommend the following:

➤ A really big skillet: I developed a lot of the recipes in this book in a 14-inch All-Clad stainless steel skillet, which is bigger than the largest pan that most home cooks own. This size allows me to cook in big batches without crowding the pan. You don't necessarily need to buy an All-Clad, which are wonderful but pricey, but I do recommend sticking with a good-quality stainless steel pan. Whatever you do, don't buy anything with a nonstick Teflon coating. Once it's scratched or worn, you don't know what chemicals are leeching into your food.

➤ Chef's knife: This is the only style of knife that I use, for all my kitchen jobs. I use an 8-inch chef's knife for everyday tasks, and a 10-inch version for slicing meat and fish. I like a knife with a good, sharp tip, and a blade wide enough

that you can use the side of it for smashing garlic. There are many good brands out there. Remember to sharpen it every 2 to 3 months.

➤ An electric knife sharpener: I sharpen my knives every couple of months on an easy-to-use electric knife sharpener made by Chef's Choice. Most professional chefs will tell you that the

only way to get a good edge is by sharpening a knife on an old-fashioned whetstone, but I think that purist perspective is a little silly, and that the results I get from my electric sharpener are every bit as good (or better). Having your own sharpener saves you the hassle of sending knives out to be sharpened, and ensures

that your blades are always in good working order.

➤ My favorite tower grater: I have an inexpensive 11-inch stainless steel tower grater made by a brand called Progressive—you can find it on Amazon—which I love because it has grating surfaces with much larger holes than your standard grater (in fact, you can't make my Confetti Gratin, page 211, properly without it). I also find its pyramid shape, strength, and size to be superior to standard box graters.
Here's the rest of the equipment that I use regularly:

➤ Convection oven: Convection ovens use a fan to distribute heat, which means they cook food faster and are very effective at developing a dry, crusty surface quality. You can convert any recipe for convection by decreasing the stated oven temperatures by 25 degrees and cooking the food for about 10 percent less time.

➤ Medium skillet: A 10-inch stainless steel skillet is the smallest size I use.

➤ Large saucepan: I've found a 4-quart stainless steel saucepan to be just the right size to handle a wide range of jobs.

➤ Wok: I love cooking in a stainless steel wok because the heat distribution is excellent, and the shape is very conducive to tossing ingredients as they cook. You can use a wok practically any time a large skillet is called for, except for when searing big pieces of meat.

➤ Dutch oven: Le Creuset is the best-known maker of enameled cast-iron Dutch ovens, which are great for making stocks, soups, braises, and stews. Staub and Lodge also make good products. I have a really big 9-quart version, but standard 5- and 6-quart sizes are also fine (you can use a stockpot for larger projects).

➤ Roasting pan: Get a nice, big one—mine is 12 x 16 inches and made from stainless steel—because it's always better to have a little too much space in the pan than too little.

➤ A 9 x 13-inch baking dish: I prefer white ceramic, because it looks good for serving. Glass also works.

➤ A 9-inch pie pan: I use Pyrex, but metal is also fine.

➤ Mixing bowls: I like lightweight, no-frills stainless steel bowls that are as wide and shallow as possible. Ideally, the largest of the bowls would be about 15 to 16 inches in diameter and 5 to 6 inches deep, with medium and small bowls as well. Get two of each size. These are easy to find at a restaurant supply store.

➤ Food processor: I like Cuisinart but there are several good brands. The standard model, which has an 8-cup capacity, is the perfect size for most of these recipes (if your work bowl is too large, it

can be hard to get traction when working with smaller quantities of ingredients). I also like my "big boy" Cuisinart, with a 16-cup capacity, for times when I'm cooking for a crowd.

➤ Immersion blender: It doesn't need to be fancy. A single-speed Cuisinart will do the trick. If you don't have an immersion blender but have a regular standing blender, that can be used instead.

➤ Baking sheets: I like really large sheet trays—ideally as big as will fit in your oven—made from stainless steel, which can withstand wear and tear and cleaning in the dishwasher. Aluminum sheet pans don't hold up so well.

➤ Salad spinner: Farmers' market produce tends to be full of grit from the field, and the best way to wash (and dry) delicate lettuces and herbs is with a spinner.

➤ Spice (/coffee/nut) grinder: The cheapest models are usually just fine.

*These tend to break so have a backup on hand*

➤ Cutting board: Get a nice, big, wooden one.

➤ Mesh colanders: These are good for everything from straining sauces to rinsing vegetables to draining pasta. Ideally, get a set of three or four in graduated sizes for different size jobs.

➤ Tongs: Buy a basic pair made from stainless steel. Don't get fancy with silicone grips or any other frills.

*Really need about 3 of these*

➤ Wooden spoon: This is the best all-purpose tool for stirring.

➤ Metal spatula: Use this for flipping items on the stove top.

➤ Fish spatula: This thinner, smaller metal spatula is ideal for working with delicate items like fish, or for getting crispy skin to release from the pan.

➤ Silicone baking spatula: Use this for mixing and scraping out bowls and pans. Be sure to get one made of silicone, which is heat resistant, since you'll use it on the stove top.

➤ Whisk: Look for a good-quality balloon whisk with plenty of wire loops for maximum whisking efficiency.

➤ Slotted spoon: You'll need this for fishing ingredients out of hot water or oil.

➤ Citrus reamer: Look for a wooden version that can be used to tackle lemons, limes, or larger citrus.

➤ Metal citrus juicer: This little metal tool— just a semicircular press attached to a handle— is the most efficient way to hand-juice big quantities of citrus fruits. They come in lemon, lime, and orange sizes, so buy according to your needs (for smaller juicing jobs, a reamer works well).

➤ Kitchen shears: Get a good pair of scissors for trimming herbs, cutting up poultry, and opening packages.

➤ Meat thermometer: Go with a digital model, since analog ones can be a pain to calibrate.

➤ Microplane grater: This is the best tool for zesting citrus and finely grating cheese.

➤ Small stainless steel paddle grater: Use this for small cheese-grating jobs where getting out a whole tower grater seems like overkill.

➤ Measuring cups: Stainless steel versions are the most durable.

➤ Measuring spoons: Ditto the above.

➤ Pint-size Pyrex measuring cup: This is useful when you're measuring volumes larger than 1 cup.

➤ White serving platters: I like to serve food on platters rather than in bowls—even dishes like potato salad—because they look more elegant that way. Look for something nice and wide.

LAMB GYROS

The Recipes

## THE RECIPES THAT FOLLOW REFLECT THE WAY THAT I COOK FOR MY FAMILY.

Most cookbooks are organized as a collection of stand-alone recipes, but *Pure Food* is organized into "threads": recipes that can be used multiple times as building blocks for several different dishes. This is how I cook at home. As a working dad, I don't have an hour and a half to spend every single evening getting dinner on the table. I take my home cooking time in chunks, and prepare things that will last in the fridge and can be used to create multiple meals throughout the week. That's how this book works.

My recipes yield big portions. This not only means that the same beef or turkey or pork recipe can be used for several different meals but also that there's always leftovers in the fridge so that my kids can graze on high-quality food, not store-bought snacks, when I'm not around to prepare a meal for them.

This book contains a lot of homemade condiments and sauces. I've learned over the years that one of the big advantages of cooking in a restaurant kitchen is having these things at your fingertips in order to put really flavorful dishes together quickly, and I've tried to bring that model home with me. I practically always have homemade sriracha (page 67) and Nutty Cheesy Breadcrumbs (page 75) on hand, to toss into dishes when I need them. Store-bought sauces and condiments are almost always filled with additives, so I hope you'll invest some time filling your fridge and freezer with these homemade flavor boosters.

Scattered among the recipes, I've also included short essays to tell you a little bit about my food businesses and some of the food producers I admire. These are intended to give you a window into some of the more common places where additives hide, and how to avoid them. A couple of additional notes before you dive in:

► Salt: All of the recipes that call for kosher salt were made using Morton brand salt. If you buy Diamond brand, another popular kosher salt, be aware that it's less dense, so you may want to add slightly more to the recipe.

► Beecher's Cheeses: Some of my recipes call for specific cheeses made by my company, Beecher's. They're available for sale at our Seattle and New York stores, or online at www.beecherscheese.com. If it's not practical for you to get your hands on these specific cheeses, here are my recommendations for substitutes, and look for high-quality, artisan cheeses whenever possible.

**BEECHER'S FLAGSHIP:** Cheddar
**BEECHER'S SMOKED FLAGSHIP:**
    Smoked Gouda or smoked cheddar
**BEECHER'S MARCO POLO:** Cheddar, plus
    1/8 to 1/4 teaspoon freshly ground black
    pepper for every 4 ounces of cheese
**BEECHER'S DUTCH HOLLOW DULCET:**
    Havarti or Monterey Jack

*Don't be afraid of waste. If you are eating clean there will be some.*

Staples + Condiments

# THE BUTCHER'S TABLE SEASONING BLEND

We use this seasoning mix in all of our restaurants whenever we're looking for an umami boost. I rely on it heavily for my **PAN-SEARED RIB-EYE** (page 115) and **ROASTED MUSHROOMS** (page 215), and also use it in **BRAISED PORK SHOULDER** (page 131), **ROASTED CAULIFLOWER** (page 196), **FARRO CAKES WITH BACON AND PARSLEY** (page 184), and several other recipes. To be honest, I would probably throw a pinch into half the recipes in this book when making them at home. I love the stuff! I recommend making a double or triple batch a couple of times a year, but this recipe makes enough to cook your way through this book once.

Do not substitute onion or garlic "powder" for the granulated version called for here. The former often contains anticaking agents. Also, I prefer the texture of the slightly larger granules to fine powder. This seasoning blend is intended to have some texture to it, so be careful when pulsing the rosemary and seeds in the coffee grinder not to process them too finely.

*(handwritten margin note)* Eggs, Soup, salad Dressing, French Fries— I could go on...

1 tablespoon dried rosemary

1 1/2 teaspoons anise seed

1 1/2 teaspoons fennel seed

2 tablespoons plus 1 teaspoon granulated garlic

2 tablespoons granulated onion

**MAKES 3/4 CUP**

2 tablespoons granulated lemon peel

2 tablespoons kosher salt

1 tablespoon plus 2 teaspoons black pepper

1 tablespoon plus 1 teaspoon chili powder

2 teaspoons Lapsang Souchong tea (2 tea bags)

**1.** Using a coffee grinder, pulse the rosemary, anise, and fennel 3 to 6 times, until most of the seeds are cracked.

**2.** In a small bowl, combine with the remaining ingredients and store in an airtight container for up to 6 months.

---

### PRO TIP

Lapsang Souchong is a Chinese smoked black tea that is available in specialty tea stores, Asian markets, and some supermarkets. Most tea bags contain crushed leaves. If you purchase whole leaf tea, pulse them in a coffee grinder into small pieces before combining with the remaining seasoning ingredients.

# OVEN-DRIED GRAPES

Drying grapes in the oven concentrates them into sweeter, chewier versions of themselves—something in between a grape and a raisin. They're great on their own as a snack, tossed into salads, or made into **ROASTED GRAPE SALSA** (page 65). I prefer using a mixture of red and green grapes, for visual appeal, because purple grapes look almost black after drying. If you're using more than one type of grape, be sure to segregate them on separate sheet trays as they may dry at different rates.

**MAKES ABOUT 2 CUPS**

3 pounds seedless grapes, mixed colors and cut in half through the stem end
2 teaspoons expeller-pressed safflower oil
1/4 teaspoon kosher salt

**1.** Preheat the oven to 200 degrees.

**2.** Toss the grapes with the oil and salt and arrange cut side up on a baking sheet. Roast in the oven until the grapes shrink by half, 4 to 5 hours. (Be sure to remove the grapes before they become chewy.)

**3.** Cool and store in an airtight container in the refrigerator for up to 3 days.

# ROASTED GRAPE SALSA

This recipe contains a lot of fresh herbs, which means it functions more or less like a salad when served alongside cooked meat. I like to pair it with **CURRIED LEG OF LAMB** (page 121), but I have also tossed it with cooked grains like farro, wheat berries, and bulgur, and with French lentils for a nutrient-dense packed lunch.

**MAKES 4 CUPS**

2 cups Oven-Dried Grapes (page 64)
1 bunch fresh flat-leaf parsley, chopped (about 2 cups)
1 bunch fresh mint leaves, chopped (about 1/4 cup)
5 tablespoons seasoned rice vinegar
5 tablespoons extra-virgin olive oil
1/4 cup capers
1/4 red onion, thinly sliced (about 1/4 cup)
3/4 teaspoon kosher salt
1/8 teaspoon black pepper

In a medium bowl, toss all of the ingredients together and either serve immediately or store refrigerated for up to 2 days.

**PRO TIP**

Make it a day ahead
for the best flavor.

# 4-YEAR FLAGSHIP AIOLI

Beecher's Extra Aged Flagship cheese ages for at least two years longer than our Flagship, giving it an intense flavor, extra sweetness, and lots of tyrosine crystals (the crunchy bits found in well-aged cheeses like Parmigiano-Reggiano). If you can't get your hands on the cheese, you can substitute high-quality, extra-sharp Cheddar. Use this aioli as a spread for sandwiches, as a dip for raw or steamed veggies, or as a creamy salad dressing. If your food processor comes with a small work bowl attachment, use it. If your food processor is larger than 8 cups and you don't have a small work bowl attachment, double the recipe to ensure that you have enough volume to create an emulsion.

**MAKES 1 1/2 CUPS**

2 egg yolks
1 tablespoon lemon juice
1 teaspoon Dijon mustard
1/2 teaspoon kosher salt
1 cup expeller-pressed safflower oil
2 tablespoons water
3 cloves Roasted Garlic (page 76), smashed into a paste
1 teaspoon Tabasco
3/8 teaspoon black pepper
1/3 pound Beecher's 4-Year Extra Aged Flagship cheese
   (page 66 for alternate), crumbled (about 1 1/2 cups)

**1.** Place the yolks, lemon juice, mustard, and salt in a food processor and process to combine, scraping down the sides and bottom of the bowl as necessary. With the processor running, very slowly stream in the first 2 to 4 tablespoons of oil. If done correctly, the oil and other ingredients should create an emulsion that appears thicker. Allow the processor to run for 1 minute before slowly streaming in the remaining oil and water, processing until fully combined and thickened like mayonnaise.

**2.** Add the remaining ingredients and pulse until just combined but not pureed, leaving visible bits of cheese for texture. (Add more water, as needed, to achieve the desired texture.)

**3.** Store in an airtight container in the refrigerator for up to 1 week.

---

### PRO TIP

......................................................

If you're using this to accompany meat and can find fresh horseradish, add 1 to 2 finely minced teaspoons of it to the recipe.

# RED FRESNO SRIRACHA

*(As seen on page 60)* Sorry, all you rabid fans of Huy Fong sriracha (also known as "rooster sauce" for the bird that decorates its bottle): that stuff is anything but pure! It contains potassium sorbate and sodium bisulfate as preservatives, plus xanthan gum as a thickener. But, don't panic. I developed this recipe for homemade sriracha for Samuel Adams using their Boston Lager and fell in love with it. I always have the spicy condiment in my fridge and typically make a quadruple batch, since my family uses it on just about everything. The vinegar and chiles are natural preservatives, which means you can keep the sriracha stored in the refrigerator almost indefinitely. Not only is this version additive-free, but it's also just plain better than the Huy Fong stuff.

When reducing the acidic beer/vinegar mixture, be sure to use a pan that will not react with acid (I prefer stainless steel). Avoid reactive materials like copper or aluminum, as the acid can degrade them and taint the flavor of your food.

**MAKES 1 1/2 CUPS**

1 (12-ounce) can Samuel Adams Boston lager, or similar rich, malty beer
1/4 cup white vinegar
1 tablespoon sugar
1 tablespoon kosher salt
8 red Fresno chiles (about 8 ounces), divided
4 cloves garlic, divided, with 2 peeled
1 teaspoon expeller-pressed safflower oil

*hoppy beers will make this taste too bitter*

1. Preheat the oven to 500 degrees.

2. In a large, nonreactive saucepan, bring the beer, vinegar, sugar, and salt to a boil. Cook for 7 minutes over high heat, then reduce the heat to medium and continue cooking for about 8 more minutes or until the liquid has reduced to 1/2 cup. Stirring occasionally, watch carefully or reduce the heat toward the end to prevent scorching. Remove the pan from the heat and set aside.

3. In a small bowl, combine 4 of the chiles, the 2 garlic cloves with skin on, and the oil. (For a spicier sauce, don't seed the chiles.)

Stir to coat and spread the mixture evenly on an ungreased baking sheet. Roast until the chile skins are blistered and blackened in places, about 7 minutes. Remove from the oven and set aside.

4. While the peppers are roasting, stem and seed the remaining 4 chiles and place with the remaining 2 peeled garlic cloves in a food processor. When the roasted peppers and garlic are cool enough to handle, stem and seed the peppers, leaving the skin on, and peel the garlic cloves. Add both to the food processor, along with the reserved beer reduction. Process the mixture until smooth.

## BEECHER'S HANDMADE CHEESE

I STARTED BEECHER'S BECAUSE I LOVE GOOD CHEESE AND COULDN'T FIND ANY BEING MADE NEAR MY HOME IN SEATTLE. This was back in 2001, and artisan cheesemaking hadn't taken off yet in the United States. Almost all the good cheeses still came from 6,000 miles away in Europe. One day, I was walking through Pike Place Market and saw a vacant storefront that I thought would be perfect for a cheese company. So, I decided I'd start one.

People thought I was crazy. The dairy industry was consolidating and creameries were going out of business, not setting up shop. As a matter of fact, we were able to buy most of the equipment that we needed for Beecher's out of bankruptcy auctions. But I'm a stubborn guy and I wasn't deterred.  >>

There are two major elements that separate artisan cheese like Beecher's from cheap, industrially produced products. The first is the quality of the milk we use; the second is the fact that we do as much as possible by hand, the way cheese has been made for thousands of years.

We spent a lot of time at the beginning lining up the right source of milk, which is absolutely critical to good cheese. We got into the cheese business at a time when most dairies were giving their cows a hormone called rBST to increase lactation (few farmers use it today, because they've found it shortens the life span of their animals). Focusing in on the few farmers we could find who said no to rBST led us to folks who valued sustainable practices the way we did, and cared more about quality than quantity.

Searching for the right breed of cattle shrunk our supplier pool further. Most milking operations use Holstein breed cows, which produce lots of sweet, low-fat, bright white milk—perfect for the milk you buy in cartons at the store, but not quite fatty enough to make a really great cheddar. I knew I wanted a decent proportion of our milk to be from another, rarer breed: the Jersey cow. Jerseys are to cows as pinot noir is to wine grapes. They're cantankerous and don't produce as much volume, but what they do produce is flavorful and nuanced and wonderful. Since Jersey milk on its own can be overwhelmingly fatty and

> It takes 10,000 pounds of milk to get about 1,000 pounds of cheese out the other end.

earthy-tasting, we use a blend of Jersey and Holstein milk for our cheese.

Today we buy from just two dairies in New York for our Manhattan store and two outside Seattle for our Pike Place store, which allows us to be very involved in and familiar with each of their farming practices. We have deep relationships with our dairies and know exactly how they treat their herds, so we don't need to rely on government certifications like Certified Organic.

We make our Beecher's Flagship cheese, an exceptionally sweet and nutty cheddar, using methods that have been around for thousands of years. We start by pasteurizing our milk. We then add a starter culture, a harmless bacteria that converts lactose into lactic acid and causes the milk to separate into curds—the fat and protein that become cheese—and liquid whey. Then we add an enzyme called rennet, which causes the milk proteins to coagulate into a gelatin-like mass. We cut the gel using handheld knives, rather than with a machine, which helps the whey begin to drain off.

Next comes the cheddaring process, where the curds are worked by hand into big blocks and stacked on top of each other, expelling more moisture. We then mill the blocks into milled curds. Salt is added, which acts as a natural preservative and halts the action of the acidifying culture. The curds are then pressed into molds overnight, expelling even more moisture, and finally allowed to age

BEECHER'S, NEW YORK

for 15 months before hitting our shelves as Beecher's Flagship cheese. It takes 10,000 pounds of milk to get about 1,000 pounds of cheese out the other end.

The process for making cheap, mass-produced cheddar looks very different. To start off with, industrial cheesemakers use commodity milk, which is collected into large pools and stored in silos. One batch of cheese might contain milk from fifty different dairies.

When large-scale cheesemakers get a shipment of milk in, the first thing they do is "standardize" it by adding milk solids or calcium chloride so that today's milk is identical in composition to yesterday's; since everything at Big Cheese is done by machine, not human hands, this type of consistency is key. They will likely use a starter culture that works as quickly as possible to convert milk into curds and whey, sacrificing depth of flavor for speed of output. They may also add a preservative such as sorbic acid or natamycin to keep mold at bay.

Traditionally, during the cheddaring process, human touch is essential in terms of adapting to the differences between batches of cheese, expelling as much moisture as possible in order to get the highest quality end result. But large cheese factories do all of this by machine. Manual labor is expensive and introduces potential for contamination.

Processed cheese, like Kraft Singles, is something else entirely. Cheese scraps are tossed together, pasteurized again, and then reconstituted with the help of emulsifiers like sodium phosphate into a cheese-like product. Various preservatives, saturated vegetable oils, acidity regulators, food dyes, milk protein concentrate, whey, and sugar usually play a role. And processed cheese lacks the good-for-you microbes present in real cheese, which promote healthy digestion. Bottom line: even if you're hard-pressed to afford true artisan cheese, avoid this stuff at all costs.

# BEECHER'S FLAGSHIP CHEESE SAUCE

Courtesy of *Pure Flavor: 125 Fresh All-American Recipes from the Pacific Northwest.*

This recipe forms the basis for Beecher's Handmade Cheese's "World's Best" Mac & Cheese. It's also great as a decadent topping for steamed veggies, and appears in **BEEF AND MUSHROOM LASAGNA** (page 105).

**MAKES 4 CUPS**

1/4 cup unsalted butter

1/3 cup all-purpose flour

3 cups milk

1 pound Beecher's Flagship cheese (page 66 for alternate), grated (about 4 cups)

1/2 teaspoon kosher salt

1/4 teaspoon chipotle chili powder

1/8 teaspoon granulated garlic

**1.** In a large saucepan over medium heat, melt the butter. Whisk in the flour and continue whisking and cooking for 2 minutes.

**2.** Slowly add the milk, whisking constantly. Cook until the sauce thickens, about 10 minutes, stirring frequently. Remove from the heat.

**3.** Add the cheese, salt, chili powder, and garlic, stirring until the cheese is melted and all ingredients are incorporated, about 3 minutes. Use the sauce immediately or store in the refrigerator for up to 3 days.

**4.** This sauce reheats nicely on the stove in a saucepan over low heat. Stir frequently so that the sauce doesn't scorch.

# CHIMICHURRI

*(As seen on page 61)* This recipe is close, but not identical, to the classic used in South America as a steak accompaniment. I like a different mix of herbs and include a chipotle pepper for a smoky, spicy kick. Feel free to customize it with whatever herbs you have available to you. While the sauce might seem acidic when tasted on its own, keep in mind that it's intended to help balance out richly flavored grilled foods.

**MAKES 2 CUPS**

1/2 cup red wine vinegar
1 dried chipotle pepper, stemmed and chopped
2 bunches fresh cilantro, chopped (about 3 cups), divided
3 large cloves garlic
1 1/2 teaspoons kosher salt
1/4 teaspoon black pepper
1 cup extra-virgin olive oil
1 bunch fresh, flat-leaf parsley, chopped (about 2 cups)
1/2 bunch fresh baby dill, chopped (about 1/2 cup)
1/2 bunch fresh mint leaves, chopped (about 1/2 cup)

**1.** In the bowl of a food processor, add the vinegar and chipotle pepper and let stand to soften the pepper, about 5 minutes.

**2.** Add 1 cup of the cilantro, garlic, salt, and black pepper and process until smooth.

**3.** Add the oil and all remaining herbs, and pulse until coarsely chopped. (A key visual for doneness is when the liquid starts to look well combined with the herbs.)

# NUTTY CHEESY BREADCRUMBS

At Liam's in Seattle, we top **ROASTED BRUSSELS SPROUTS** (page 195) with these breadcrumbs. This crunchy topping packs big flavor, making it a versatile condiment for things like roasted vegetables, stir-fried greens, pastas, and stews. It's a great way to make use of day-old bread.

**MAKES ABOUT 2 1/2 CUPS**

1/4 cup hazelnuts (about 1 1/4 ounces)
2 tablespoons extra-virgin olive oil
1/4 loaf of bread, torn or cubed (about 4 ounces)
3 ounces Beecher's Flagship cheese (page 66 for alternate), grated (about 3/4 cup)

1. Preheat the oven to 325 degrees.

2. In a food processor, pulse the nuts and oil until finely chopped. Add the bread and cheese and process for about 2 minutes into rice-size crumbs. Spread the crumb mixture evenly on a rimmed baking sheet, making sure the layer is no more than 1/4 inch deep. (You may need more than one baking sheet.) Bake until golden and crisp, 20 to 30 minutes, switching and rotating the baking sheet and stirring halfway through the cook time.

3. Use immediately or cool completely and store in an airtight container at room temperature for up to 3 days.

*I make these at home and keep a small bowl of them next to my salt. They keep a long time out in the open. And add a tasty crunch/cheesy richness to lots of stuff.*

# ROASTED GARLIC

This method is the fastest way to achieve the mellow/sweet flavor of roasted garlic needed for recipes like **ANCHO ROASTED CARROTS** (page 197) and **4-YEAR FLAGSHIP AIOLI** (page 66). It works well for one clove or forty, and though the cloves won't be quite as sweet and soft as in a slow-roasted garlic recipe, they will add a nice, mellow garlic flavor to the dishes listed.

Cloves garlic, separated but left unpeeled

Preheat the oven to 375 degrees. Place the unpeeled garlic cloves on a baking sheet and bake for 15 minutes, until softened. Cool slightly, peel, and either use immediately or store in the refrigerator for up to 1 week.

# 2-HOUR QUICK KIMCHEE

This is ideally suited for the **PORK BIBIMBAP** (page 133), but I've also offered this as a topping to the **LAMB GYROS** (page 122) and **BEEF HASH** (page 99). Check your local Asian grocer for the gochugaru, a Korean chili powder, though you can use regular chili powder in a pinch.

**SERVES 6**

1/4 head red cabbage, sliced thin and cut into 1- to 2-inch pieces (about 3 cups)
6 tablespoons seasoned rice vinegar
2 tablespoons gochugaru (Korean chili powder)
1 tablespoon kosher salt
2 teaspoons The Butcher's Table Seasoning Blend (page 63 )

In a large bowl, mix together the cabbage, vinegar, gochugaru, salt, and The Butcher's Table Seasoning Blend until well combined. Refrigerate for 2 hours, stirring every 30 minutes or so. Serve cold or at room temperature. The kimchee can be stored for up to 3 days in the refrigerator.

# TOMATILLO AVOCADO SALSA VERDE

*(As seen on page 60)* This is like the Reese's Peanut Butter Cup of salsa recipes. It marries the richness of guacamole with the brightness of tomatillo sauce, and together they make a versatile sauce that can be used as a dip or condiment. This recipe makes enough salsa for **TURKEY BURRITOS AHOGADOS** (page 141), plus a bonus 1 1/2 cups to be used later in the week.

**MAKES 3 1/2 CUPS**

2 poblano chiles (about 10 ounces)
6 fresh tomatillos, husks and stems removed, cut into quarters
2 avocados, halved, seeded, and flesh spooned out from skin
2 jalapeño peppers, stemmed, seeded, and roughly chopped
1 cup roughly chopped fresh cilantro
2 tablespoons expeller-pressed safflower oil
1 1/2 teaspoons lime juice
1 1/2 teaspoons kosher salt

**1.** Using tongs and a gas burner (or the oven; see note), roast the poblanos, turning occasionally, until charred in spots but not blackened all over. (The pepper will not be completely cooked through, still having some firmness to it when done.) When cool enough to handle, remove the stems and seeds, but leave the skin on.

**2.** In a food processor, pulse the poblanos and remaining ingredients into a chunky puree. The salsa verde can be stored for up to 2 days in the refrigerator.

**NOTE:**

If you don't have a gas burner, preheat the oven to 500 degrees. Toss the chiles with 1 to 2 teaspoons expeller-pressed safflower oil to lightly coat and place on a baking sheet. Roast until the skin is blistered all over and blackened in spots, 6 to 10 minutes.

*These are really really good!*

# OVEN-DRIED TOMATOES

Long, slow oven drying concentrates tomatoes into sweeter and more flavorful versions of themselves. Their texture is softer than that of a sun-dried tomato, but meatier than a raw or stewed tomato. This versatile ingredient can be served alongside eggs, on salads, or on sandwiches. Chop and add them to potato or pasta salad, or simply toss them into hot pasta with kalamata olives and fresh herbs. These tomatoes are also an integral component in my **SPICY OVEN-DRIED TOMATO SAUCE** (page 81) and pair nicely with **FARRO CAKES WITH BACON AND PARSLEY** (page 184). I prefer using Roma (aka plum) tomatoes, but practically any tomato will do. Cherry or grape varieties make for a tarter, lighter variation, but be sure to scale the cooking time down to account for their smaller size and faster drying time.

**MAKES ABOUT 1 1/3 POUNDS**

3 pounds (12 to 15) plum tomatoes, cut crosswise into 3 round pieces

4 teaspoons extra-virgin olive oil, plus more for storing (4 to 16 tablespoons)

1/4 teaspoon kosher salt

**1.** Preheat the oven to 200 degrees. Line a baking sheet with parchment paper.

**2.** Evenly distribute the tomatoes in one layer, cut side up, on the baking sheet. (You may need more than one baking sheet.) Drizzle 4 teaspoons of the olive oil and sprinkle salt over the cut surfaces of the tomatoes.

**3.** Roast in the oven until the tomatoes shrink by half, 4 to 6 hours. Remove from the oven and either serve immediately or set aside to cool.

**4.** To store, put the cooled tomatoes in an airtight container with enough olive oil to cover. Refrigerate for up to 2 weeks. Return to room temperature before serving.

### PRO TIP

Use the tomato-enriched storing oil as a finishing oil or base for salad dressing.

# RICH ROASTED TOMATO BEEF STOCK

We're looking to make a super savory stock here, without the use of MSG or other artificial flavor enhancers that many restaurants and food companies use to get their broths tasting rich and satisfying. Tomato paste is naturally rich in glutamates and boosts the umami character of this stock. Browning the bones in a hot oven helps amp up their richness and extracts the most flavor from them. I call for "meaty" beef bones in this recipe: that means bones with a decent quantity of flesh still stuck to them. This stock is ideal for use in **THREE-ALARM BEEF CHILI** (page 108) and **FRENCH DIP ROAST BEEF SANDWICH WITH AU JUS** (page 96 ).

**MAKES 8 CUPS**

6 tablespoons expeller-pressed safflower oil
1 1/2 tablespoons tomato paste
1 teaspoon kosher salt
1/4 teaspoon black pepper
5 pounds meaty beef bones or short rib ends
4 quarts water

1. Preheat the oven to 450 degrees.

2. Whisk the oil, tomato paste, salt, and pepper in a large bowl. Add the bones and toss to coat.

3. Spread the bones evenly between two baking sheets. Roast in the oven, turning the bones over once halfway through the cooking time, until deeply browned and slightly blackened in some spots, 12 to 15 minutes.

4. Transfer the bones to a large pot and cover with the water. Bring to a boil over high heat, reduce the heat to low, and maintain a simmer for 4 to 8 hours, or until reduced by half and the stock tastes meaty. (You can simmer overnight, if the heat is low enough.)

5. Using a mesh strainer, strain the stock into a large container, discarding the solids, and either use right away or cool to room temperature before storing. Before using, defat the stock. To defat hot stock, use a ladle, wide spoon, or fat separator. If you are not using the stock right away, refrigerate the stock to cool. After the stock has been refrigerated, the fat hardens on the surface and is very easy to remove with a spoon. The stock can be stored in the refrigerator for 1 week or frozen for up to 6 months.

---

### PRO TIP

If all your butcher has to sell you is clean bones, buy a combination of bones and short ribs. (If you ask for the end cut ribs, your butcher just might give you a discount.)

# SPICY OVEN-DRIED TOMATO SAUCE

This recipe combines canned tomatoes and oven-dried fresh ones to create a rounder, more complex flavor than either would provide on its own. The anchovy paste adds depth, as well as the necessary salt to balance the brightness of the tomatoes. This ultra-savory sauce can be used in any recipe that calls for tomato sauce, but the heat and balanced acidity really shine in the **POLENTA VERDURE** (page 175) and **BEEF AND MUSHROOM LASAGNA** (page 105).

Although it's well worth the effort to make your own, there are reasonably good store-bought tomato sauces available. Due to their high acidity, tomatoes lend themselves to canning without the use of any additional preservatives (although, unfortunately, almost all add sugar of some kind). Look for sauces labeled just "tomato sauce" or "marinara," without additions like meat, cream, or vegetables. You can make a double batch of this recipe and freeze half for future uses.

**MAKES 6 CUPS**

2 tablespoons extra-virgin olive oil
4 medium cloves garlic, crushed and roughly chopped
    (about 2 tablespoons)
2 teaspoons dried oregano
1 1/2 teaspoons red pepper flakes
1 1/2 cups white wine
1 pound Oven-Dried Tomatoes (page 78), removed from oil
    (about three-fourths of one recipe)
1 (28-ounce) can crushed tomatoes
1 tablespoon anchovy paste
1 teaspoon kosher salt
1/4 teaspoon black pepper

**1.** In a large saucepan over medium-high heat, cook the olive oil, garlic, oregano, and red pepper flakes, stirring occasionally, until fragrant, about 1 minute. Add the wine and cook over high heat until the mixture is reduced by half, about 5 minutes.

**2.** Remove the saucepan from the heat and add the dried tomatoes, canned tomatoes, anchovy paste, salt, and pepper. Using an immersion blender, pulse the mixture into a rustic puree. Alternatively, if you don't have an immersion blender, blend or process the tomatoes in a standing blender or food processor before adding them to the saucepan. Return the sauce to a boil and either use immediately or cool and store in the refrigerator for up to 1 week or the freezer for up to 3 months.

# TZATZIKI

Tzatziki is a cool, tangy yogurt-based sauce from Greece. I pair it with **LAMB GYROS** (page 122), but feel free to use it as a sandwich spread, alongside salads and grilled meats or vegetables, or as a dip. English cucumbers are drier and meatier and have fewer seeds and thinner skins than standard cucumbers. If you can't find one, be sure to peel and seed your standard cucumber before grating.

**MAKES 1 1/2 CUPS**

1 1/2 cups plain, whole milk Greek yogurt
1/2 English cucumber, coarsely grated (about 1 cup)
1 tablespoon capers, mashed and roughly chopped
1 tablespoon chopped fresh mint
1 tablespoon chopped fresh dill
1 teaspoon lemon juice
1 teaspoon dried oregano
3/4 teaspoon kosher salt
1/2 teaspoon granulated garlic
1/2 teaspoon black pepper
1/2 teaspoon lemon zest (from 1/4 lemon)

Mix all the ingredients together in a medium bowl. Either serve immediately or store for up to 3 days refrigerated in an airtight container.

# CRISP PROSCIUTTO

Prosciutto baked to a crisp in the oven is beautiful and dramatic left whole, but also excellent broken into shards for topping salads or as a lower-fat bacon substitute. At my Seattle restaurant Liam's, we top each Liam's Burger with one crisp slice.

Slices of prosciutto

Preheat the oven to 350 degrees. Evenly space the slices of prosciutto on a parchment-lined or oiled baking sheet. Bake until mostly crisp, about 13 minutes. Remove from the oven and allow the prosciutto to cool on the baking sheet, at which point the slices should be crisp all the way through.

# QUICK PICKLED RED ONIONS

*These keep forever and can add a dash of color to practically anything*

(*As seen on page 61*) I'm not the biggest fan of raw onions because of their gastric and breath side effects. This recipe gives you all the crunch and punch of raw onions without the lingering aftertaste. When you first add the raw onions to the liquid, they might not fully submerge. As they pickle, they will collapse into the liquid. The longer you marinate them, the more vibrantly red they become. Ideally, let the onions pickle for 24 hours before serving.

**MAKES 2 CUPS**

2/3 cup red wine vinegar
2/3 cup water
1 tablespoon kosher salt
1/2 teaspoon sugar
1 medium red onion, thickly sliced into 1/4- to 1/2-inch rings (about 1 cup)

Mix together the vinegar, water, salt, and sugar in a medium bowl. Microwave the mixture until steaming, about 1 minute. Add the onions, mix, and set aside. When cooled, cover and refrigerate until ready to use. (The onions can be prepared up to 2 weeks before using.)

# SERRANO CHILE BBQ DIPPING SAUCE

*(As seen on page 60)* Beer is a classic BBQ sauce starter, and I recommend selecting a quality lager for this recipe. The sauce gets its smoky flavor from the inclusion of chipotle powder and Lapsang Souchong tea. These ingredients can be found at Latin and Asian markets, respectively, or ordered online. If you can't find Lapsang Souchong, omit the ingredient entirely rather than substituting a different type of tea. This recipe, as is, is medium spicy. Adding or subtracting two serranos will take you down to mild or up to hot. And leftovers will keep in your refrigerator practically forever.

**MAKES 4 CUPS**

1 1/2 teaspoons Lapsang Souchong tea (about 1 teabag)
1 1/2 teaspoons expeller-pressed safflower oil
1 yellow onion, chopped (about 1 1/2 cups)
2 serrano chiles, chopped
6 cloves garlic, minced
3/4 cup beer (1/2 bottle), preferably lager
1 (15-ounce) can crushed tomatoes
1 1/2 cups pineapple juice
5 ounces cider vinegar
1/3 cup molasses
1 1/2 teaspoons chipotle chili powder
1 1/2 teaspoons red pepper flakes
1 1/2 teaspoons kosher salt

**1.** Cut open the bag of tea and pour the tea leaves into a small bowl, discarding the bag. Set aside.

**2.** Preheat a large saucepan over medium-high heat. Add the oil, followed by the onion and chiles. Sauté, stirring frequently, until softened and browned, about 10 minutes. Add the garlic and cook until fragrant, about 2 minutes.

**3.** Add the tea and the remaining ingredients. Bring the mixture to a boil, then reduce the heat to low and simmer, stirring occasionally, until reduced to 4 cups, about 50 minutes.

**4.** Puree using an immersion blender. Alternatively, if you don't have an immersion blender, blend or process the sauce in a standing blender or food processor before returning it to the saucepan.

**5.** Keep warm until ready to serve.

# ESCABECHE

Similar to the canned or jarred jalapeños often served with nachos, these spicy, pickled vegetables work well as a complement to Mexican dishes, chopped and added to omelets, or served as part of an antipasti plate. They keep almost indefinitely in your refrigerator.

**MAKES 3 CUPS**

5 cups water, divided
6 ounces carrots, cut into 1/4-inch pieces on the bias
  (about 2 medium-large carrots)
1/2 white onion, quartered and cut into 1/4-inch slices
2 jalapeño peppers, sliced
1 cup white vinegar
2 teaspoons kosher salt

**1.** In a large saucepan, bring 4 cups of the water to a boil. Add the carrots, reduce the heat to medium-low, and simmer until the carrots just barely give, about 3 minutes. Strain the carrots and rinse under cold water to slightly cool and transfer to a bowl. Add the onion and jalapeños.

**2.** In a small saucepan, bring the vinegar, remaining 1 cup water, and salt to a boil. Pour over the vegetables and let cool. Cover and refrigerate for at least 1 hour before using.

# LURA'S CURRIED HAZELNUTS

My longtime executive sous chef and recipe collaborator, Lura Smith, came up with this recipe to serve as a bar snack and cheese accompaniment at Beecher's Cellar in New York City. These hazelnuts are crunchy, savory, sweet, and infuriatingly addictive. The egg whites help the spices adhere to the nuts, and ensure that they become super crunchy.

**MAKES 1 POUND (ABOUT 3 1/4 CUPS)**

1 egg white
1 pound raw hazelnuts, skins on
6 tablespoons sugar
1 3/4 teaspoons kosher salt
1/2 teaspoon ground cumin
1/2 teaspoon ground coriander
1/4 teaspoon ground ginger
1/4 teaspoon chili powder
1/4 teaspoon black pepper
1/8 teaspoon cayenne

**1.** Preheat the oven to 325 degrees.

**2.** In a large bowl, whip the egg white with a whisk until frothy. Add the hazelnuts and stir to coat. In a small bowl, combine the sugar, salt, and spices until evenly mixed. Sprinkle the spice mixture over the nuts and stir until evenly coated.

**3.** Spread the nuts evenly on a parchment-lined baking sheet and bake until dry and crisp, 25 to 35 minutes, rotating the sheet halfway through the baking time. Remove from the oven and cool completely on the baking sheet.

**4.** Break the hazelnuts apart and serve. They can be stored in an airtight container for 3 weeks.

### PRO TIP

Wrapped up in little bags, these are great for holiday gift giving.

# POBLANO RELISH

*(As seen on page 60)* As with pickles, most store-bought relishes are filled with additives. Common ones include high fructose corn syrup (which is sometimes the second ingredient), added flavors, artificial dyes, emulsifiers, preservatives, and thickeners. So, making my own relishes is a top priority, both at home and in my restaurants. This easy homemade version is great on tacos, as a sandwich spread, or as a base for other sauces and dips (imagine a spoonful stirred into guacamole). Roasting the chiles and including the charred skin adds smoky depth to its bright, vinegary flavor profile.

**MAKES 1 1/2 CUPS**

4 poblano chiles (about 20 ounces), divided
1 jalapeño pepper
1 medium clove garlic, smashed and roughly chopped
1 teaspoon kosher salt
1/4 cup seasoned rice vinegar
3 tablespoons expeller-pressed safflower oil

**1.** Using tongs and a gas burner (or in the oven; see note), roast the poblanos and jalapeño, turning occasionally, until the skin is blistered all over and charred in spots. When cool enough to handle, remove the stems and seeds and roughly chop.

**2.** In a food processor, add one-third of the chopped chile and jalapeño mixture and the garlic, salt, vinegar, and oil, and puree until smooth. Add the remaining chile mixture and pulse until a chunky puree forms (like pickle relish). The relish can be stored refrigerated in an airtight container for up to 1 week.

**NOTE:**
If you don't have a gas burner, preheat the oven to 500 degrees. Toss the chiles with 1 to 2 teaspoons expeller-pressed safflower oil to lightly coat and place on a baking sheet. Roast until the skin is blistered all over and blackened in spots, 6 to 10 minutes.

*The color of this fades a little after the first day. But the flavor actually gets better!*

# UPPER EAST SIDE STEAK SAUCE

*a wonderful, adventure!*

*(As seen on page 229)* I wrote this cookbook <u>during the year I spent living on the Upper East Side</u> of New York City. The neighborhood is known for having residents who expect the best of the best, and this recipe is just that: a perfect sauce for steak, and so much more. Mushrooms are naturally high in umami-building glutamates, and chiles, sautéed onion, and garlic all work to amplify this sauce's savory punch. Put together, these ingredients will keep you and your family from missing additive-filled bottled steak sauces.

This recipe relies on high-heat cooking to build flavor. Be sure to have all ingredients ready to go and to "clear the decks" for 10 minutes while you focus on cooking.

**MAKES 2 CUPS**

1/4 cup expeller-pressed safflower oil

1/2 jalapeño pepper, stemmed, seeded, and cut into thin strips

1/2 yellow onion, diced (3/4 to 1 cup)

2 tablespoons white vinegar

2 teaspoons finely chopped ancho chile (about 1/4 chile)

12 ounces mushrooms, sliced 1/8-inch thick

1 1/2 teaspoons kosher salt

1 clove garlic, minced (about 1 teaspoon)

**1.** In a large skillet over high heat, heat the oil until smoking, about 1 minute. Add the jalapeño and cook, without stirring, until the pepper is just beginning to blacken on one side, about 2 minutes. Add the onion and cook until the onion is translucent, about 3 minutes. Add the vinegar and ancho chile and cook until partially reduced, 1 minute. Add the mushrooms, salt, and garlic, and cook, stirring occasionally, until the mushrooms release their moisture and partially collapse, about 3 minutes.

**2.** Serve immediately or store refrigerated in an airtight container for up to 5 days; rewarm before serving.

# WINTER PESTO

Pesto doesn't always have to be made from basil, pine nuts, and Parmesan. This wintry version is based around my recipes for **ROASTED MUSHROOMS** (page 215) and **RED FRESNO SRIRACHA** (page 67). Boldly flavored kalamata olives, arugula, pistachios, and smoked cheese make this sauce powerful enough to use with heartier grains (farro is my favorite) and whole grain pastas. Plan for 2 cups of pesto per pound of pasta or grain. Alternatively, consider serving this pesto as an antipasti dip, or as a condiment for simply cooked fish or vegetables.

**MAKES 3 1/2 CUPS**

1 recipe Roasted Mushrooms (page 215), roughly chopped
28 kalamata olives (about 4 ounces), pitted
4 ounces Beecher's Smoked Flagship cheese (page 66 for alternate), roughly chopped or grated (about 1 cup)
2 ounces baby arugula (about 2 cups packed)
1 ounce shelled pistachios (about 3 tablespoons)
1/2 cup Red Fresno Sriracha (page 67)
1/2 cup extra-virgin olive oil

Place all ingredients in a food processor and pulse into a chunky puree. The pesto can be stored for up to 3 days in the refrigerator.

EYE OF ROUND
ROAST

Beef

# EYE OF ROUND ROAST

*(As seen on page 92-93)* Eye of round is an inexpensive cut with a nice, even shape that makes carving a breeze. You can serve this roast the day it's cooked with the accompanying pan sauce alongside vegetables and starches of your choosing (be sure to use the browned bits stuck to the sheet tray after roasting to pack the pan sauce with the maximum flavor). Leftovers can be shaved thinly into sandwich meat for **FRENCH DIP ROAST BEEF SANDWICH WITH AU JUS** (page 96) or chopped and made into **BEEF HASH** (page 99) or **BEEF AND PEPERONATA CROSTINI** (page 100). Salting the meat ahead of time is worth the extra effort, and the longer the better, as it ensures a juicier finished product.

**SERVES 4 TO 6
WITH LEFTOVERS
FOR AT LEAST ONE
OF THE ABOVE
RECIPES**

1 teaspoon granulated garlic
1 teaspoon chili powder
1 tablespoon kosher salt, plus more to taste
1 teaspoon finely chopped fresh rosemary
1/2 teaspoon black pepper, plus more to taste
5 pounds eye of round, trimmed
2 tablespoons unsalted butter, softened
2 tablespoons all-purpose flour
2 cups Rich Roasted Tomato Beef Stock (page 80), divided

**1.** In a small bowl, mix together the garlic, chili powder, salt, rosemary, and pepper. Sprinkle the mixture evenly over the entire surface of the meat. Wrap the seasoned meat tightly in plastic and refrigerate for 4 to 24 hours.

**2.** Preheat the oven to 500 degrees.

**3.** Roast the meat on an oiled baking sheet until browned on the exterior, 25 to 30 minutes, flipping the roast using tongs and a spatula halfway through. Remove the meat and reduce the oven temperature to 300 degrees. Return the meat to the oven and continue to roast until the center registers 115 degrees for medium-rare, 35 to 40 minutes.

**4.** Using tongs and a spatula, transfer the meat to a carving board, setting the baking sheet aside, and allow to rest for 30 to 45 minutes before slicing and serving.

**5.** Meanwhile, work the softened butter and flour into a smooth paste in a small bowl using a spoon or fork. Add 1/2 cup stock to the baking sheet and scrape up any browned bits with a spatula. Pour this enriched stock into a saucepan with the remaining 1 1/2 cups stock and bring to a boil over medium-high heat. Add the butter mixture and whisk to fully combine and thicken, 1 to 3 minutes.

**6.** Strain the sauce through a fine-mesh strainer. Add salt and pepper to taste. (The sauce can be served immediately or rewarmed at mealtime in a microwave or on the stove top.)

**7.** Serve the thinly sliced roast with the warm pan sauce.

# FRENCH DIP ROAST BEEF SANDWICH WITH AU JUS

The French Dip, a sandwich consisting of thinly shaved beef, cheese, and savory dipping sauce, is my idea of the ultimate roast beef sandwich. Mine uses an "au jus" sauce based off **RICH ROASTED TOMATO BEEF STOCK** (page 80); the secret is to add just a couple tablespoons of **SERRANO CHILE BBQ DIPPING SAUCE** (page 85) for depth and subtle, smoky sweetness. Be sure to shave the beef as thinly as possible, using a sharp knife. It's okay if the slices aren't perfect rounds, as they will be folded and layered like deli meat when assembled. The **4-YEAR FLAGSHIP AIOLI** (page 66) takes this sandwich over the top, and eliminates the need for additional cheese.

Whatever you do, don't substitute deli counter roast beef for the homemade version. Deli meats are absolutely lousy with additives and preservatives, including cancer-causing nitrates and nitrites, BHA or BHT, binders, meat tenderizers, thickeners, emulsifiers, corn syrup, MSG, phosphates, and color fixatives. Avoid at all costs!

**SERVES 6**

1 tablespoon expeller-pressed safflower oil
2 shallots, chopped (about 1 cup)
2 1/2 cups Rich Roasted Tomato Beef Stock (page 80)
4 cloves Roasted Garlic (page 76), smashed
3 sprigs fresh flat-leaf parsley
1 sprig fresh thyme
3/4 teaspoon kosher salt, plus more to taste
2 tablespoons Serrano Chile BBQ Dipping Sauce (page 85)
6 brioche buns
6 tablespoons 4-Year Flagship Aioli (page 66)
30 ounces Eye of Round Roast (page 94), thinly shaved
1/2 recipe Quick Pickled Red Onions (page 84), drained (about 1/2 cup)

**1.** To make the au jus, in a large saucepan over medium-high heat, heat the oil until shimmering, 1 to 2 minutes. Add the shallots and cook until just softened, about 3 minutes. Add the stock, garlic, parsley, thyme, salt, and BBQ sauce, and bring to a boil. Reduce the heat to medium-low and simmer until the liquid is reduced by half and slightly thickened, about 20 minutes.

Strain the au jus through a fine-mesh strainer set over a small saucepan, discarding the solids. Season to taste and cover, keeping it warm until ready to serve.

**2.** Assemble the sandwiches on the brioche buns with the aioli, beef, and pickled onions divided evenly among the 6 buns. Serve alongside the au jus.

# BEEF HASH

Hashes make for great brunches or casual dinners. While any cubed or shredded cooked meat will do, this recipe is designed to use up leftover **EYE OF ROUND ROAST** (page 94). For a more decadent version, serve this hash topped with a poached egg or a sprinkling of cheese.

**SERVES 4 TO 6**

1 1/2 pounds small Yukon gold potatoes (1 to 2 inches in diameter)
6 tablespoons unsalted butter, divided
1 medium fennel bulb, halved and sliced into
   1 x 1/2-inch strips (about 2 cups)
2 1/2 teaspoons kosher salt, divided
1/2 teaspoon black pepper, divided
2 teaspoons lemon juice
3 tablespoons capers, drained
1 large shallot, diced (about 1/2 cup)
2 teaspoons smoked paprika
1 tablespoon dried oregano
12 ounces Eye of Round Roast (page 94), chopped into 1/2-inch pieces
4 whole jarred piquillo peppers, chopped (about 1/2 cup)
1 ear corn, kernels cut from cob
1/2 bunch fresh flat-leaf parsley, roughly chopped (about 1 1/2 cups)

**1.** Place the potatoes in a large bowl, cover, and microwave until the potatoes are tender, 10 minutes, redistributing halfway through cooking. Meanwhile, in a large skillet, melt 1 tablespoon of the butter over medium-high heat. Add the fennel, 1/2 teaspoon salt, and 1/4 teaspoon black pepper. Cook, stirring occasionally, until tender and well browned, 3 to 5 minutes. Add the lemon juice and stir to coat. Transfer the fennel to a bowl and wipe the skillet clean.

**2.** Using the side of a chef's knife, smash the cooked potatoes into 1/2-inch-thick disks. Halve or quarter each disk depending on the size of the potato.

**3.** Return the skillet to medium-high heat and melt the remaining 5 tablespoons butter. Add the capers, shallot, paprika, and oregano and cook until fragrant, about 1 minute. Add the potatoes and the remaining 2 teaspoons salt and stir, flipping the potatoes, to coat evenly with the butter mixture. Cook, without stirring, until the potatoes are browned on the bottom, 3 to 5 minutes. Fold in the cooked fennel and remaining ingredients until evenly combined. Cook until warmed through, about 5 minutes, and serve.

Beef

# BEEF AND PEPERONATA CROSTINI

These crostini are packed with flavor and beautiful enough to serve at cocktail parties or as dinner party appetizers. They're a great way to repurpose leftovers, if you have **EYE OF ROUND ROAST** (page 94), **RED CABBAGE PEPERONATA** (page 202), and **4-YEAR FLAGSHIP AIOLI** (page 66) on hand.

**SERVES 4 TO 6**

1/2 hearty country bread loaf, sliced 1/2 inch thick and cut into about 1 1/2 x 4-inch pieces (about 1/2 pound)

2 tablespoons extra-virgin olive oil

12 ounces Eye of Round Roast (page 94), cut into 1/2-inch cubes

1 cup Red Cabbage Peperonata (page 202), roughly chopped

3/4 cup 4-Year Flagship Aioli (page 66)

1. Preheat the broiler.

2. Brush each slice of bread with oil on one side. Place the slices on a baking sheet, oiled side up, and toast under the broiler until they are lightly browned, 1 to 3 minutes.

3. Toss the beef and peperonata together and set aside. Spread the toasts with aioli and then top with the beef/peperonata mixture. Serve immediately.

I serve these with and without the beef. Super Tasty both ways. Be careful not to make the bread *too* crunchy or they are hard to eat.

# BRAISED BEEF CHUCK ROAST

Chuck roast—which comes from the cow's shoulder—is one of the most underrated cuts of beef. I love it because it's both cheaper and beefier-tasting than most common cuts. Braising makes the most of its meaty flavor and dissolves its collagen into gelatin, rendering a tough piece of meat tender.

This braise yields robustly flavored liquid that can easily be transformed into a sauce using a French culinary technique called *beurre manié*. Although it sounds fancy, it requires nothing more than mixing a paste of flour and softened butter into warm liquid just before serving. In addition to being great on its own, this is the base recipe for **THREE-ALARM BEEF CHILI** (page 108) and **BEEF AND MUSHROOM LASAGNA** (page 105).

**SERVES 6 TO 8, OR 4 WITH ENOUGH LEFTOVERS TO MAKE THREE-ALARM BEEF CHILI OR BEEF AND MUSHROOM LASAGNA**

5 pounds beef chuck, fat trimmed and beef cut into 1-inch cubes
3 tablespoons expeller-pressed safflower oil
1 tablespoon chopped fresh rosemary
2 teaspoons kosher salt, plus more to taste
1 tablespoon whole green peppercorns,
    ground in spice grinder or pepper mill, plus more to taste
1/2 teaspoon black pepper
1 teaspoon granulated garlic
1 teaspoon chili powder
1 cup water, divided
2 tablespoons unsalted butter, softened
2 tablespoons all-purpose flour

**1.** Preheat the oven to 500 degrees.

**2.** In a large bowl, toss the beef with the oil, rosemary, salt, green and black pepper, garlic, and chili powder until evenly coated. Evenly spread between two ungreased baking sheets, making sure the pieces are not touching. Roast the beef until browned, 20 to 30 minutes.

**3.** Reduce the oven temperature to 300 degrees. Place the beef pieces in a large roasting pan. Add 1/2 cup of the water to each baking sheet and scrape with a spatula or wooden spoon to release any browned bits. Transfer this liquid and any released bits to the roasting pan with the beef. Cover the roasting pan with foil and bake in the oven until the beef is easily pierced with a fork, about 2 hours. Remove the meat from the roasting pan and set aside.

**4.** Strain the liquid into a bowl and use a wide spoon to skim the fat from the surface. (Optionally, place in the refrigerator until chilled and then remove the hardened fat from the surface.) The meat and the braising liquid can be stored in the refrigerator for several days and reheated to serve. (If you are making this recipe to use the beef in other recipes, you do not need to continue on to the next steps of reheating and creating a gravy.) When ready to serve, if the meat has been chilled, preheat the oven to 325 degrees, put the meat into a roasting pan, and sprinkle with a few tablespoons of the braising liquid. Cover with foil and bake for 10 to 20 minutes.

**5.** Just before serving, place 2 cups braising liquid (or braising liquid plus enough water to equal 2 cups) in a saucepan over medium heat. Meanwhile, work the butter and flour into a smooth paste in a small bowl using a spoon or fork. When the liquid is simmering, add the butter paste and whisk to combine. Continue whisking and cooking for 1 minute, until the sauce is slightly thickened and the paste is fully incorporated. Season with salt and ground green peppercorns to taste. Serve immediately alongside the warm meat.

# BEEF AND MUSHROOM LASAGNA

This lasagna is deeply satisfying, packed with meaty pieces of braised beef and roasted mushrooms and accented with a velvety cheese sauce. Topping (rather than baking) with tomato sauce adds bright contrast to this rich dish. Lasagna almost always tastes better the day after it's made. I recommend making it 1 to 3 days ahead and portioning it while cold. Reheat individual portions, spaced out on a sheet tray, in a 350-degree oven for about 12 minutes (or until warmed through). Top it with warmed tomato sauce and herb salad (recipe follows) before serving.

Use the **ROASTED MUSHROOMS** (page 215), **ROASTED ONIONS** (page 194), **BRAISED BEEF CHUCK ROAST** (page 102), **BEECHER'S FLAGSHIP CHEESE SAUCE** (page 72), and **SPICY OVEN-DRIED TOMATO SAUCE** (page 81) recipes for this lasagna. If you can't find fresh lasagna noodles, precook dried ones according to the package instructions. You might end up with extra noodles; only use what is necessary to create a single sheet thickness for each layer.

**SERVES 6 TO 8**

4 cups (about 1 recipe) Beecher's Flagship Cheese Sauce (page 72), divided

1 pound fresh lasagna noodles, trimmed to fit a 9 x 13-inch baking dish, divided

1 recipe Roasted Mushrooms (page 215), roughly chopped

1 recipe Roasted Onions (page 194), roughly chopped

1 1/2 pounds Braised Beef Chuck Roast (page 102), fat and connective tissue removed, meat shredded and roughly chopped

2 ounces Beecher's Flagship cheese (page 66 for alternate), grated (about 1/2 cup)

4 1/2 cups Spicy Oven-Dried Tomato Sauce (page 81)

*Really any leftover braised beef could work here*

1. Preheat the oven to 350 degrees.

2. Using a spatula, spread 1/2 cup cheese sauce evenly over the bottom of a lightly greased 9 x 13-inch glass or ceramic baking dish. Place one layer of pasta over the sauce, covering the entire surface.

3. Layer all of the mushrooms evenly over the pasta, followed by the onions. Pour 1 cup cheese sauce evenly over the vegetables and use a spatula to spread to the edges.

4. Place a second layer of pasta over the sauce. Top the noodles with the beef. Pour 1 cup cheese sauce over the beef and use a spatula to spread to the edges. Place the final layer of pasta over the sauce. Pour the  >>

remaining 1 1/2 cups of cheese sauce over the pasta and use a spatula to spread evenly to the edges. Top with the grated cheese.

**5.** Bake until bubbling and the cheese is browned, 40 to 60 minutes, depending on your lasagna's thickness. Allow to rest for 10 minutes before serving.

**6.** To serve, place a portion of lasagna in each bowl. Top each portion with tomato sauce. Serve immediately.

# HERB SALAD

**MAKES 3 CUPS**

3 cups mix of herbs and peppery greens (like parsley, basil, watercress, and arugula), torn or chopped into bite-size pieces
1 tablespoon lemon juice
1/8 teaspoon kosher salt

In a large bowl, gently toss the herbs with the lemon juice and salt.

# THREE-ALARM BEEF CHILI

We Dammeiers like our food spicy, and this chili has been a longtime favorite for the heat it packs. If you prefer a more mellow heat, reducing the quantity of chipotle chile powder will tone it right down. This recipe comes together in no time if you have leftover **BRAISED BEEF CHUCK ROAST** (page 102) on hand. Just omit the beef chuck and substitute 2 pounds of leftover chuck roast, with the meat shredded and the fat and connective tissue removed. After adding the stock, reduce the simmer time from 2 hours down to 10 minutes. Feel free to get creative with your garnishes. I've listed a few recommendations below, but don't be timid; let the contents of your fridge be your guide.

**SERVES 4 TO 6**

3 pounds beef chuck, trimmed and cut into 1-inch cubes

4 tablespoons expeller-pressed safflower oil, divided

4 teaspoons kosher salt, divided

1/2 cup water

2 red onions, chopped (about 1 1/2 cups)

2 white onions, cut into large dice

2 jalapeños, minced

2 poblanos, seeded and diced

4 medium cloves garlic, smashed and minced

1 tablespoon ground cumin

1 tablespoon dried oregano

1 tablespoon chili powder

2 tablespoons chipotle chili powder

1 recipe Rich Roasted Tomato Beef Stock (page 80)

1 (28-ounce) can crushed tomatoes

1/4 cup apple cider vinegar

1 teaspoon honey

2 to 4 tablespoons masa flour (as needed)

**OPTIONAL GARNISHES (2 TABLESPOONS PER SERVING):** coarsely grated Beecher's Flagship cheese (page 66 for alternate) or Dutch Hollow Dulcet cheese, diced onion, chopped fresh cilantro

1. Preheat the oven to 500 degrees.

2. Toss the beef with 2 tablespoons of the oil and 2 teaspoons of the salt. Roast the meat on a baking sheet until well browned, 20 to 30 minutes. Remove from the oven and transfer the meat to a medium bowl. Add the water to the baking sheet to deglaze, scraping any browned bits from the bottom of the sheet. Pour the water mixture into the bowl with the meat.

3. While the beef is cooking, in a stockpot over high heat, heat the remaining 2 tablespoons oil until smoking, 1 to 2 minutes. Add the onions, jalapeños, poblanos, and remaining 2 teaspoons salt and cook, stirring occasionally, for 10 minutes, until the vegetables are softened and starting to brown. Add the garlic, cumin, oregano, chili powder, and chipotle chili powder and cook, stirring constantly, until fragrant, about 1 minute. Add the stock, tomatoes, vinegar, and honey and cook, scraping any browned bits from the bottom of the pot. Add the meat and deglazing liquid to the stockpot. Bring the mixture to a boil, reduce the heat to medium-low, and simmer until tender, about 2 hours.

4. If the chili broth appears thin, sprinkle the masa flour evenly over the surface of the chili and whisk in. Return to a boil and let thicken to your desired consistency. Serve hot, garnishing each bowl individually.

---

**PRO TIP**

I'm not entirely sure why, but chili almost always tastes spicier right when it's made than it does a few hours, let alone a few days, later.

## MISHIMA RESERVE

I BROUGHT MISHIMA RESERVE INTO
THE SUGAR MOUNTAIN FAMILY IN 2013,
because I believe that the brand is doing
something different and better than what
passes for quality in America's broken beef
cattle industry. Mishima Reserve specializes
in raising and selling American Wagyu beef.
Wagyu is a breed of cattle native to Japan,
famous around the world for its tender,
healthy, beautifully marbled meat.

Thanks to selective breeding, Wagyu
cattle have a different body composition
than other types of cattle, like the Angus
and Herefords traditionally raised in the
U.S. They have a unique ability to store fat
within their muscle tissue, meaning their
meat is far more tender and flavorful than
even the best prime cuts produced from
other types of cattle. Wagyu also contain
half the level of saturated fat and twice the
level of monounsaturated fat—a lighter,
sweeter, healthier fat—than other breeds do.
They have higher levels of healthy omega-3
and omega-6 fatty acids as well.  >>

Shane Lindsay started Mishima Reserve in 2005, intent on giving America broader access to this incredible meat. A third-generation cattleman from California, Shane spent time in Japan as a young man learning the ins and outs of cattle farming. Back in the States, he was hired by the premium beef company Agri Beef to help them raise Wagyu cattle. Initially, all this ultra-premium meat was shipped back to Japan, where the market was hungry for as much Wagyu as possible. But by the end of the 1990s, American chefs had begun to discover the amazing eating quality of the breed, and the company began to sell the beef domestically under the brand name Snake River Farms.

Despite all his success at Snake River Farms, Shane decided to strike out on his own. He wanted a small, very integrated operation that would allow him to see the cattle through from beginning to end, ensuring a high level of quality and transparency.

Beef cattle production in the United States is a very segmented industry, making it impossible for any one person to know with certainty exactly how an animal was treated through the whole chain from birth, through its life, up to the time when it's processed and distributed. There's one operation that supplies bulls for mating, and another that owns the cow and the calf she gives birth

to. The calf is bought by a third operation, a feedlot, and grown as quickly as possible to slaughter weight. The animal is then sold to a big meatpacker to slaughter, butcher, process, and pass off to a distributor, who then sells the meat into restaurants and retail stores. Each of these entities knows next to nothing about the ones above and below it in the chain; a career rancher might not be able to tell the difference between choice and prime grade beef, and a processor couldn't necessarily identify an Angus breed cow out of a lineup.

Mishima Reserve does things differently. We've integrated the whole system, so that we can say with confidence what a steer's genetic makeup is and how it was raised, guarantee that it was slaughtered humanely, and processed without the use of any added chemicals.

Beyond breeding cattle with a better capacity for marbling, we also raise the cattle with more care. Most cattle in the United States are raised with the goal of maximizing efficiency; our goal is to maximize the truly great genetic potential of our superior Wagyu bloodlines.

So while most cattle are forced to put on weight as quickly as possible and harvested between 18 and 20 months of age, we grow them over the course of 24 to 30 months. This allows them to put weight on slowly, the way nature intended. After we start them on grass, they are finished on grains.

> Wagyu contain half the level of saturated fat and twice the level of monounsaturated fat—a lighter, sweeter, healthier fat—than other breeds do. They have higher levels of healthy omega-3 and omega-6 fatty acids as well.

PAN-SEARED RIB-EYE WITH THE BUTCHER'S TABLE SEASONING BLEND

We tailor their feed specifically for this gradual program of weight gain, giving them less corn than most cows and more barley, alfalfa, and wheat straw.

It won't surprise you to hear that Mishima Reserve has a zero tolerance policy for additives of any kind. Many American cattle are fed antibiotics, not just when they're sick, but as a part of their normal diet to fend off any of the illnesses that will inevitably be caused by overcrowded living conditions. They are also given hormones to speed their weight gain. After processing, the meat might be treated with gases to keep it pink, or injected with a solution of salt, water, flavorings, and preservatives to make it seem juicy and fresh over the course of a long shelf life. Mishima Reserve never, ever does any of those things. And since we control the process from start to finish, consumers can have peace of mind knowing that their beef is 100 percent additive-free.

# PAN-SEARED RIB-EYE WITH
# THE BUTCHER'S TABLE SEASONING BLEND

**THE BUTCHER'S TABLE SEASONING BLEND** (page 63) really brings out the meaty flavor of this premium cut of beef. I recommend serving it with **UPPER EAST SIDE STEAK SAUCE** (page 90) and a savory mushroom accompaniment to deliver the ultimate umami bomb. Alternatively, you can dress it with **CHIMICHURRI** (page 73) for a brightly acidic/herbal counterpoint to the steak's richness. I usually make **SMASHED POTATOES** (page 207) as a side dish, for my family's version of a meat and potatoes dinner.

**SERVES 2 TO 4**

2 boneless rib-eye steaks (1 1/2 to 2 pounds)
2 tablespoons expeller-pressed safflower oil, divided
2 teaspoons The Butcher's Table Seasoning Blend (page 63),
   or 1 teaspoon per pound of meat
1/2 teaspoon kosher salt
1/4 teaspoon black pepper

**1.** In a large bowl, toss the steaks with 1 tablespoon of the oil, The Butcher's Table Seasoning Blend, salt, and pepper, until thoroughly and evenly coated. Cover and place in the refrigerator for 1 to 24 hours (longer is better). Remove from the refrigerator 30 minutes before cooking to bring to room temperature.

**2.** Preheat the oven to 325 degrees.

**3.** In a large skillet, heat the remaining 1 tablespoon oil over high heat until smoking. Add the steaks and cook until well browned on one side, 5 minutes. Flip the steaks and immediately transfer the steaks to the oven, keeping them in the skillet. Cook the steaks to your preferred doneness. (For rare, cook to 115 degrees when tested with a meat thermometer, about another 5 minutes.)

**4.** Remove the steaks from the skillet and let rest for 5 minutes. Slice the steaks thinly on the bias and serve immediately.

---

### PRO TIP

Ask your butcher for rib-eyes cut from the "loin end" to get more regularly shaped steaks with less connective tissue.

# BENNETT'S BURGERS

This burger has been on the menu at Bennett's in Seattle since day one. Many customers tell us it's the best burger they've ever had. I absolutely love pork, and adding just a little bit rounds out the flavor without it starting to taste like a sausage. **THE BUTCHER'S TABLE SEASONING BLEND** (page 63) was originally developed for these burgers, and we have subsequently realized that it's great for just about anything that can benefit from a savory punch. Use a delicate touch when mixing and shaping burgers to prevent them from becoming tough; leaving the edges rough (versus evenly shaped and smooth) means more edge surface area for browning and flavor.

Serve, as we do at Bennett's and Liam's, topped with Beecher's Flagship cheese (page 66 for alternate), **QUICK PICKLED RED ONIONS** (page 84), and **CRISP PROSCIUTTO** (page 84) on a toasted brioche bun spread with a 50/50 blend of grainy mustard and mayonnaise.

**MAKES 4
BURGER PATTIES**

1 1/2 pounds ground beef
1/2 pound ground pork
2 tablespoons The Butcher's Table Seasoning Blend (page 63)

1. In a large bowl, lightly mix the meats and seasoning until just combined.

2. Divide into 4 portions. Gently shape each portion into loose, 3/4-inch-thick patties with rough edges. Make the centers of the patties 1/2 inch thinner than the edges. Set aside until ready to cook, up to 30 minutes at room temperature or up to 24 hours in the refrigerator.

3. Grill (or cook indoors in a skillet) to desired doneness and serve.

Lamb

**NOTE:**
Don't be shy when trimming away connective tissue. Expect to lose about 25 percent of the roast's weight during this process.

# CURRIED LEG OF LAMB

This recipe requires some up-front investment in terms of butchering time, but the benefits are many: smaller pieces of lamb will cook faster and taste better than one large roast, due to the increased surface area for browning and rubbing with spices. When portioning the lamb, aim for pieces that are roughly rectangular (rather than square) in shape and 1 1/2 to 2 inches thick. I like to serve this dish with **ROASTED GRAPE SALSA** (page 65) and/or **CHIMICHURRI** (page 73) spooned directly over the meat, plus **ROASTED CAULIFLOWER** (page 196) on the side, but it's worth making just to have the meat for <u>**LAMB GYROS**</u> (page 122).

*I REALLY like the gyros and it's worth doing this just for them*

**SERVES 8**

4 tablespoons expeller-pressed safflower oil, divided
1 tablespoon kosher salt
3 tablespoons curry powder
1 tablespoon ground cumin
1 tablespoon dried oregano
2 teaspoons cayenne
2 teaspoons granulated garlic
1/2 teaspoon black pepper
4 pounds boneless leg of lamb, trimmed of connective tissue
   and portioned into 6- to 8-ounce pieces

1.  Combine 2 tablespoons of the oil, salt, and all of the spices in a large bowl. Add the lamb and toss to coat evenly. Cover and refrigerate for 3 to 24 hours.

2.  Preheat the oven to 425 degrees.

3.  In a large skillet over high heat, heat the remaining 2 tablespoons oil until smoking. Working from the thickest to the thinnest pieces, add the meat to the hot pan one at a time, waiting 10 seconds between adding each piece. This helps the pan maintain a searing heat. (If you put all of the meat in the pan at the same time, it will cool the temperature of the pan.) Cook until browned all over, 4 to 8 minutes, turning as necessary. Transfer the skillet to the oven and continue cooking until done, 5 to 8 minutes longer. (For rare, cook to 120 degrees when tested with a meat thermometer.) Remove individual pieces from the oven to a carving board as each one achieves doneness.

4.  Rest the meat for 10 minutes before thinly slicing and serving.

# LAMB GYROS

Use leftover **CURRIED LEG OF LAMB** (page 121) for this quick weeknight meal. As you prep the meat, be sure to remove any remaining chewy connective tissue. Feel free to substitute any type of flatbread for the pita used in the below recipe. I am especially fond of a Norwegian flatbread called lefse, but naan or even a large tortilla will do. **TZATZIKI** (page 83) and **QUICK PICKLED RED ONIONS** (page 84) are integral to these gyros, but don't hesitate to get creative with other vegetable and sauce accompaniments. Consider passing **RED FRESNO SRIRACHA** (page 67) tableside for an added kick.

**SERVES 4 TO 6**

1 pound leftover Curried Leg of Lamb (page 121), thinly sliced and roughly chopped
1 cup fresh cilantro leaves
1/2 English cucumber, chopped
1 medium carrot, coarsely grated
1/3 cup drained Quick Pickled Red Onions (page 84), roughly chopped
4 to 6 pitas
Tzatziki (page 83)

Mix the lamb, cilantro, cucumber, carrot, and onions together in a large bowl. Place each pita on a piece of foil (see note), leaving the top inch or two exposed. Stuff the lamb mixture into the pitas, topping with tzatziki. Wrap the pita in foil and serve, passing additional tzatziki at the table.

**NOTE:**
Alternatively, you can use wax or parchment paper. The foil or paper keeps the gyros from falling apart while assembling and eating.

RIDGE
80% ZINFANDEL, 11% CARIGNANE
1% ALICANTE BOUSCHET
PRODUCED BY RIDGE VINEYARDS
BOTTLED BY RIDGE VINEYARDS

# RIDGE VINEYARDS

DURING HIS NEARLY FIFTY YEARS MAKING WINE AT RIDGE VINEYARDS, Paul Draper has followed one simple philosophy: that the taste of a wine should reflect the vineyard it came from, and the grapes and yeast that live there, with minimal intervention from the winemaker. In Paul's view, the best vineyard sites have no need of modern additives to produce fine wines.

It's an idea that sits in stark opposition to the methods popular among winemakers today, many of whom hold degrees in oenology—the chemistry and biology of winemaking—and typically alter the wine they make using a host of additives and processing methods.  >>

Some sixty additives are permitted for use in wine in the United States and worldwide, among them stabilizers, clarifying agents, acidifying agents, concentrates, preservatives, and chemical sterilizers (for instance, an antimicrobial called Velcorin, highly toxic in its undiluted form, is permitted for use in wine and fruit juices and kills everything in the product). A dozen different invasive processing machines can be used to manipulate the beverage as well; reverse osmosis machines, for example, force wine through a membrane at high pressure to remove vinegar, excess sugar, and alcohol—and a lot of the liquid's flavor subtleties along with them.

"Modern winemaking allows the winemaker to 'create' the wine using processing and additives to result in whatever he or she decides is a 'good' wine," Paul explains. "From my point of view, with grapes from a fine vineyard, that approach alters the quality and character of what could have been a fine wine."

Paul's interest in wine began when he was in high school on the East Coast, but it was while studying at Stanford in the mid-1950s that he began devoting himself to sampling fine wines from California and Europe. Before long, it dawned on him that the best wines he tasted were the ones produced before industrial winemaking techniques came into general use.

"The wines made in the mid- to late 1930s were the finest California wines I had ever tasted, far more complex than the '50s and '60s, and comparable to the best Bordeaux

wines of the '40s and '50s," Paul said. "Then starting in the late '30s, the University of California at Davis began the reinvention of winemaking as an industrial process."

At Ridge, in California's Santa Cruz Mountains, wines are still made the way they were in the late nineteenth and early twentieth centuries.

It begins in the vineyards. Paul farms the estate vineyards organically—"true organic," as he puts it—which means not only avoiding conventional chemicals but also paying close attention to the microbiologic life of the soil and health of the individual vines.

The grapes at Ridge are hand-harvested, and fermented by the yeast and malolactic bacteria that come to the winery on the grapes; by contrast, the vast majority of winemakers add a range of selected commercial yeast and malolactic bacteria to ferment their grapes.

"We've limited ourselves to the very few things that have been used with fine wine for the past two hundred years," Paul explained. "We've found that we can, in fact, produce very high-quality wine without using any of these modern chemicals."

And, Ridge does something practically unheard of in the world of wine: they list their ingredients on the label.

Unlike all other packaged goods, alcoholic beverages are not required to disclose their ingredients on the packaging. When mandatory ingredient labeling first began for packaged foods, the wine and spirits industry opposed it fiercely, claiming that with natural products such as theirs, it would be impossible to predict inputs in order to include them on a label. Paul first attempted to voluntarily list all of Ridge's inputs in the early 1970s, but the federal authorities at that time wouldn't permit him to do so. Finally, several years ago, Paul was granted permission, and Ridge has voluntarily included an ingredient list on its wine labels ever since.

Despite his clean winemaking practices, the wines that Paul makes at Ridge are not organic wines. The reason has to do with sulfites. Limited amounts come from the soil, but they're also added in varying quantities during the winemaking process. Their role is to control the growth of undesirable yeast and bacteria, which if allowed to grow unchecked could seriously alter the flavor of a wine. In Paul's view, adding small quantities of sulfur dioxide, a type of sulfite, is essential to creating consistent wines that reflect the distinctive character of where the grapes were grown.

In a small percentage of people, high doses of sulfites can cause asthma-like symptoms such as wheezing and difficulty breathing. So, Paul uses what he deems to be the "minimum effective level" of sulfites in his wines, well below the amounts typically used by most vintners.

"What I've found is that if we use absolutely no sulfur dioxide, we can't consistently see the character of where the grapes were grown," Paul explained. "It's not truly fine wine. Sulfur dioxide is the one thing we have to add to be able to create consistently fine wine. It's a necessary tool."

The issue, he feels, is with the high levels of sulfites used by some producers, who want to "play it safe" and limit the potential for a wine to go "off."

Although Paul (and most winemakers) believe that it's impossible to consistently make good wine without at least some added sulfur dioxide, if you're committed to avoiding sulfites, stick with Certified Organic wine (which, in the United States, can legally contain only minuscule amounts of added sulfites). Make sure you're buying "Certified Organic" wine, not simply wine "made from Certified Organic grapes"; the latter may still use additives in the winemaking process.

Like organic wines, so-called "natural" wines are also growing rapidly in popularity. Natural wines tend to be additive-free; as with all packaged goods, there is no legal regulation of the term "natural," but the wine industry is more self-regulating on these principles than most. Because the use of sulfites is so important to preventing strange flavors in wine, the quality of natural wines varies widely, and most are meant to be consumed within a year or so of bottling.

And what about biodynamic wines? This designation, regulated by a group called Demeter, indicates that a winemaker takes a holistic, somewhat spiritual approach to agriculture. As with what Paul refers to as "true organic" practices, biodynamic vintners avoid conventional chemicals in their farming, and pay particular attention to the life and health of the soils and the vines. Biodynamic winemaking allows for the addition of sulfites in relatively small quantities, but the majority of other additives are not permitted.

BRAISED PORK
SHOULDER

Pork

It's really
tough to keep from
eating this pork right
from the pan. Like little
balls of meat cookie dough!

# BRAISED PORK SHOULDER

Pork shoulder is one of my favorite meats. It's rich and versatile, plays well with all kinds of sauces, and is practically impossible to overcook. It's also one of the few cuts that can be either braised or grilled, if cut thin enough. By cubing the pork shoulder first, you increase the surface area of the meat and thus increase the opportunity for browning while simultaneously cutting down on cooking time. Braising ensures fork-tender results and creates the base for a rich accompanying sauce. This recipe yields enough pork for eight servings. Consider serving it as a dinner for four to six one evening alongside **WILTED COLLARD GREENS** (page 213) and **SMOKY GRITS** (page 174) and then using the leftovers later in the week for **CHILE VERDE** (page 134).

**SERVES 8, OR 4 WITH ENOUGH LEFTOVERS TO MAKE CHILE VERDE**

6 pounds boneless pork shoulder, trimmed of fat (see note on page 132) and cut into 2-inch cubes

1 1/2 tablespoons The Butcher's Table Seasoning Blend (page 63)

1 tablespoon smoked paprika

2 teaspoons dried oregano

1 teaspoon black pepper, plus more to taste

1/2 teaspoon cayenne

2 teaspoons kosher salt, plus more to taste

3 tablespoons expeller-pressed safflower oil

1 yellow onion, roughly chopped (about 1 1/2 cups)

3 cups water, divided

2 tablespoons all-purpose flour

1 to 3 teaspoons cider vinegar

1. Preheat the oven to 500 degrees.

2. In a large bowl, toss the pork with the seasoning blend, spices, salt, and oil until evenly coated. Evenly spread between two ungreased baking sheets, making sure the pieces are not touching. Roast the pork until browned, about 20 minutes.

3. Reduce the oven temperature to 350 degrees. Spread the onion on the bottom of a large roasting pan. Place the pork and any juices on top of the onions. Add 1/2 cup of the water to each baking sheet and scrape with a spatula or wooden spoon to release any browned bits. Transfer this liquid and any released bits to the roasting pan. Cover the roasting pan with foil and bake in the oven until the pork is easily pierced with a fork, about 1 1/2 hours. Remove the meat from the roasting pan and set aside. >>

**4.** To make the gravy, place the roasting pan over medium heat. Evenly sprinkle the flour into the roasting pan and, using a whisk, combine the flour with the pan juices. Add the remaining 2 cups water and continue whisking to incorporate. Cook, whisking frequently, until slightly thickened, about 4 minutes. Season to taste with vinegar, salt, and pepper. Plate the pork and top with the gravy. Serve warm.

**NOTE:**

To make pork lard, heat a heavy-bottomed pan over medium heat. Roughly chop the fat and add it to the pan, evenly distributing it in one layer. Cook the fat in the pan until the fat is fully rendered, stirring occasionally, 30 to 60 minutes, depending on how much fat you start with. (When done, the fat will be well browned and there will be no translucent, visible fat.) Using a fine-mesh strainer, strain the fat and store refrigerated for up to 3 months.

---

### PRO TIP

Pork shoulder trim can be rendered into pork lard and bacon-like bits (see note) and used in Smoky Grits (page 174), Wilted Collard Greens (page 213), or to substitute for cooking oil or butter in any recipe that might benefit from a subtle pork flavor (think eggs, potatoes, beans, and stir-fries).

# PORK BIBIMBAP

When I make bibimbap, there are some specific ingredients that I like to work with because I think they yield the best texture and flavor in the finished dish. First, I prefer to use tamari soy sauce in the pork preparation. It has a richer color and flavor than the more common Chinese soy sauces, and is a little less salty. Also, I'm a big fan of gochugaru, which is a fiery Korean chili powder, but you can use regular chili powder in a pinch. Finally, for the best possible texture, shred the carrots with the 11-inch stainless steel tower grater by Progressive, available on Amazon (see page 53 for more information).

**SERVES 6**

1 1/2 pounds pork tenderloin, cut into 1-inch cubes
2 tablespoons toasted sesame oil
2 tablespoons tamari soy sauce
1 tablespoon gochugaru (Korean chili powder)
1 teaspoon kosher salt
1 teaspoon granulated garlic
1/2 teaspoon black pepper
2 cups uncooked brown rice
2 tablespoons expeller-pressed safflower oil
2 medium carrots, coarsely grated (about 2 cups)
1 recipe 2-Hour Quick Kimchee (page 76)
6 fried eggs
1 bunch cilantro, roughly chopped
Red Fresno Sriracha (page 67), to taste

**1.** In a large bowl, mix together the pork with the sesame oil, tamari, gochugaru, salt, garlic, and black pepper until the pork is evenly coated. Let marinate for 1 1/2 hours in the refrigerator. While the pork marinates, prepare the rice according to the package instructions and set aside.

**2.** When the pork is done, in a large skillet over medium-high heat, heat the safflower oil. Place the pork in the pan, making one even layer, and let cook for 1 minute. Stir, flipping each piece of pork over, and let sit for 1 minute. Stir and continue cooking for 3 more minutes, stirring until the pork is cooked to desired doneness and making sure it does not burn.

**3.** To serve, divide the rice evenly among 6 bowls. To each bowl, add a serving of pork, carrots, and kimchee. Top with a fried egg and some cilantro. Serve the Red Fresno Sriracha alongside.

# CHILE VERDE

The acidity of the tomatillos and subtle heat from poblanos and jalapeños balance the richness of the pork in this hearty stew. To ensure that the broth has some body, I whisk in a mashed avocado during the final minutes of cooking. This is a technique I started using early on at Bennett's restaurant for thickening cioppino, a hearty Italian fish stew. This Chile Verde is a great use for leftover **BRAISED PORK SHOULDER** (page 131); serve it garnished with grated Beecher's Smoked Flagship cheese (page 66 for alternate), **RED FRESNO SRIRACHA** (page 67), and/or **CHIMICHURRI** (page 73).

**SERVES 5**

2 poblano peppers

2 jalapeño peppers

2 tablespoons expeller-pressed safflower oil

3 yellow onions, chopped (about 3 cups)

12 ounces tomatillos, roughly chopped (about 9 tomatillos)

6 medium cloves garlic, roughly chopped (about 1/4 cup)

2 1/2 teaspoons kosher salt

4 1/2 cups water (for added depth of flavor, try replacing half of the water with beer)

1 large very ripe avocado, peeled, pitted, and mashed

1 1/4 pounds Braised Pork Shoulder (page 131), roughly chopped

1 bunch fresh cilantro, roughly chopped (about 2 cups)

1 ear corn, kernels cut from cob

1 red Fresno chile, stemmed, seeded, and finely diced

1 teaspoon honey

1. Using tongs and a gas burner (or in the oven; see note), roast the poblanos and jalapeños, turning occasionally, until the skin is blistered all over and charred in spots. When cool enough to handle, remove the stems and seeds from the poblanos and chop into a small dice. For the jalapeños, stem and chop into a small dice, leaving the seeds.

2. In a Dutch oven over high heat, heat the oil until smoking, 1 to 2 minutes. Add the onions and cook, stirring occasionally, until partially browned and fully translucent, 3 to 5 minutes. Add the roasted peppers, tomatillos, garlic, and salt and cook until the tomatillos collapse, 3 to 5 minutes.

3. Add the water and bring to a boil. Reduce the heat to low and whisk in the avocado. Add the pork, cilantro, corn, Fresno chile, and honey, and simmer to meld the flavors and warm through, about 5 minutes. Serve immediately or cool to room temperature before storing in the refrigerator for up to 5 days or the freezer for up to 3 months.

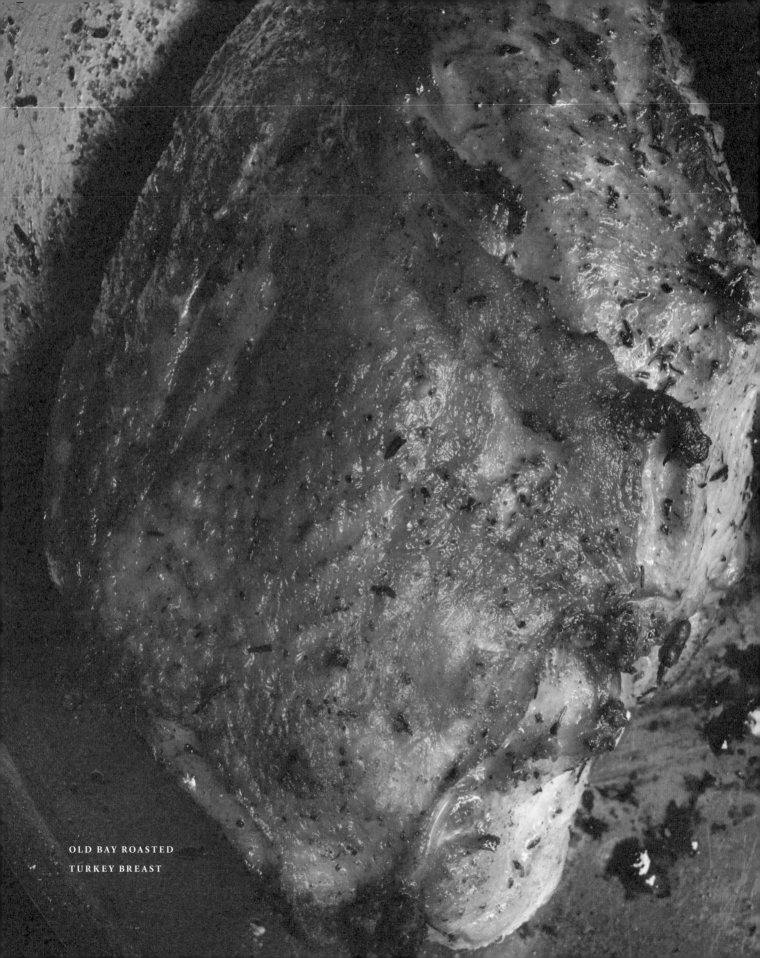

OLD BAY ROASTED
TURKEY BREAST

Turkey

# OLD BAY ROASTED TURKEY BREAST, PLUS STOCK

*(As seen on page 136-137)* Deli meats are the worst of the worst in terms of chemical enhancements and preservatives. This simple recipe will help your family avoid processed sandwich meat entirely. It gets great flavor from Old Bay Seasoning, which you may be surprised to hear is one of the few original seasoning mixes that remains all-natural and free of additives.

Turkeys are sold in a range of sizes, which means the breasts you find at the grocery store may not be the same weight as what I call for in this recipe. If the breast you end up with is smaller, simply scale down the seasoning and cooking times accordingly.

Be sure to buy bone-in breasts if you can. It may seem like a pain to have to do the butchering work yourself, but meat purchased on the bone tends to be of a higher quality than boneless versions, and will leave you with bones and trim for making Turkey Stock (recipe follows). You can ask your butcher to do this for you—just be sure you go home with the bones for making stock.

It's also good to keep in mind that these large breasts will continue cooking a bit once they leave the oven, just like larger meat roasts do. Be sure to remove them from the oven before they're fully cooked and allow them to rest before slicing and serving.

This recipe yields enough turkey for a few meals. Consider serving the freshly roasted turkey with **SPICY CHICKPEA PUREE** (page 201) and **OVEN-BRAISED FENNEL** (page 199) for the first meal, and then using the leftover turkey in sandwiches and in **TURKEY TORTILLA SOUP** (page 144) and **TURKEY BURRITOS AHOGADOS** (page 141) throughout the week.

**SERVES 12 TO 18,
OR 4 TO 6 WITH ENOUGH
LEFTOVERS TO MAKE TURKEY
TORTILLA SOUP AND TURKEY
BURRITOS AHOGADOS**

1 (13-pound) whole turkey breast (already butchered:
   about 9 pounds of boneless, skin-on breast meat)
1/3 cup expeller-pressed safflower oil
1 tablespoon Old Bay Seasoning
1 teaspoon dried thyme
1 teaspoon kosher salt
1/2 teaspoon black pepper

**1.** With the skin side of the turkey breast facing up, use the tip of your knife and a series of lengthwise shallow cuts to gently remove each breast from either side of the central breastbone and back ribs. Set the breasts aside in a large bowl. Reserve the bones for making Turkey Stock (recipe follows).

**2.** Add the oil, Old Bay Seasoning, thyme, salt, and pepper to the turkey, mixing thoroughly until the turkey is evenly coated. Cover and place the bowl in the refrigerator for 1 to 24 hours (the longer, the better).

**3.** Preheat the oven to 400 degrees. >>

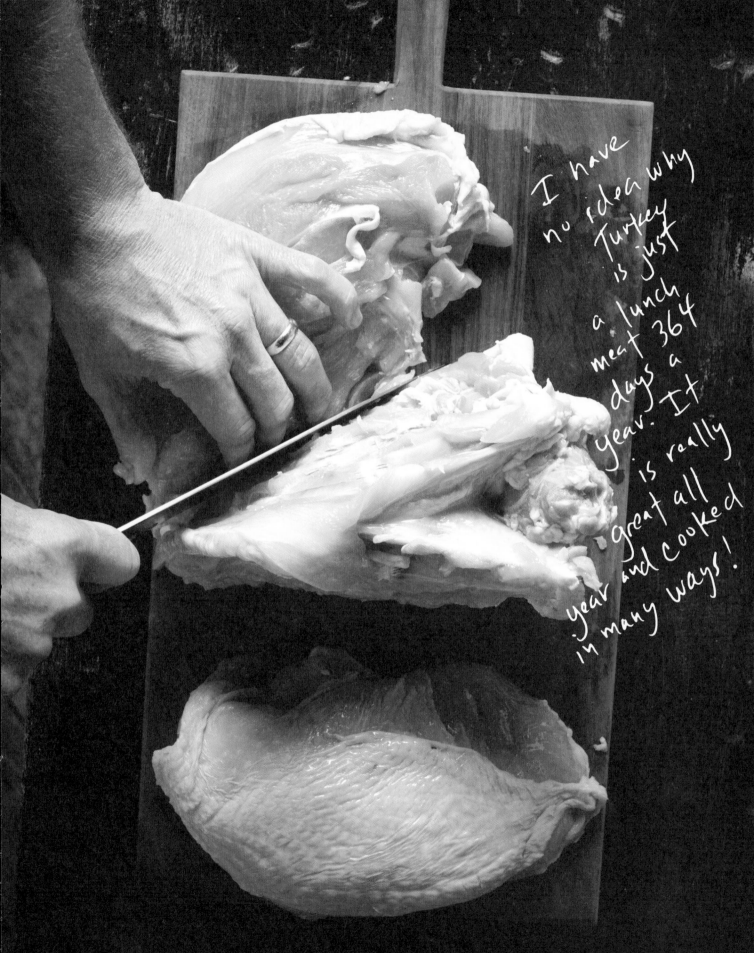

I have no idea why Turkey is just a lunch meat 364 days a year. It is really great all year and cooked in many ways!

**4.** Transfer the marinated turkey breasts, skin side up, to a roasting pan and bake for 45 minutes to 1 hour, or until tender and no longer pink. Transfer the breasts to a cutting board and let rest for 20 minutes. Cut the breasts into 1/2-inch-thick slices and serve immediately.

# TURKEY STOCK

This stock can be stored until needed and is great in **TURKEY TORTILLA SOUP** (page 144) or in any recipe that calls for chicken stock.

**MAKES ABOUT 3 QUARTS**

Turkey bones from 1 (13-pound) whole turkey breast
Pinch of salt and black pepper
1 tablespoon expeller-pressed safflower oil
1 gallon water

**1.** Preheat the oven to 425 degrees.

**2.** Using kitchen shears, cut the bones into pieces that will fit into a stockpot. In a large bowl, toss the bones with the salt, pepper, and oil. Spread the bones onto a baking sheet and roast until deeply browned, 30 to 40 minutes.

**3.** Remove the bones from the oven and transfer to a stockpot, covering with the water. Bring to a boil, reduce the heat to medium-low, and simmer until the meat falls off the bones and the liquid reduces by 20 percent, 1 to 2 hours.

**4.** Using a mesh strainer, strain the stock, discarding the solids, cool, and store in the refrigerator for up 1 week or the freezer for up to 3 months.

# TURKEY BURRITOS AHOGADOS

Someone once told me that the name of this dish—which is somewhere between enchiladas and fajitas—translates literally to "little wet donkeys," but don't let that deter you from cooking these smothered, delicious burritos. They pack big flavor. Each one is stuffed with a combination of veggies, meat, and cheese and topped with a bright tomatillo sauce. One recipe makes four burritos, each of which is large enough to satisfy up to two people. Using leftover **OLD BAY ROASTED TURKEY BREAST** (page 138) and **TOMATILLO AVOCADO SALSA VERDE** (page 77) ensures that this meal comes together quickly enough for a weeknight dinner. Consider serving them with **POBLANO RELISH** (page 89) and **ESCABECHE** (page 86) as tableside condiments.

**SERVES 4 TO 8**

2 tablespoons expeller-pressed safflower oil, divided

1 white onion, coarsely chopped

1 teaspoon kosher salt, divided

1/4 teaspoon black pepper, divided

2 medium cloves garlic, crushed and roughly chopped (about 1 tablespoon)

1 1/2 teaspoons dried oregano

1 teaspoon chipotle chili powder

1/2 teaspoon ground cumin

1 red bell pepper, cored, seeded, and thinly sliced (roughly 2 x 1/8-inch strips)

1/4 head red cabbage, shredded (about 1 1/2 cups)

6 ounces Beecher's Flagship cheese (page 66 for alternate), coarsely grated (about 1 1/2 cups)

4 ounces Dutch Hollow Dulcet, coarsely grated

2 cups Tomatillo Avocado Salsa Verde (page 77), divided

4 (10-inch) flour tortillas

1 ear corn, kernels cut from cob (about 1/2 cup)

1 pound turkey meat from Old Bay Roasted Turkey Breast (page 138), skin discarded and meat cut into bite-size cubes

3 tablespoons lime juice

---

### PRO TIP

Double this recipe and freeze half.

---

**1.** In a large skillet over high heat, heat 1 tablespoon of the oil until smoking. Add the onion, 1/2 teaspoon of the salt, and 1/8 teaspoon of the pepper and cook until the onion is charred in spots and just softened, about 3 minutes. Stir and cook an additional 1 to 2 minutes until the onion is more evenly browned. Add the garlic, oregano, chipotle chili powder, and cumin, and cook, stirring, until fragrant, about 1 minute. Transfer the onion mixture to a large bowl.

**2.** Return the skillet to high heat and add the remaining 1 tablespoon oil, heating the oil just until smoking. Add the bell pepper, the remaining 1/2 teaspoon salt, and the remaining 1/8 teaspoon pepper, and cook until the peppers are beginning to brown and are just softened, about 3 minutes. Add a third of the cabbage (setting the rest aside until ready to serve), stir to mix with the peppers, and transfer the mixture to the bowl with the onions. (The vegetables can be made through this step up to 1 day before and held in the refrigerator until you are ready to assemble the burritos and bake.)

**3.** Preheat the oven to 350 degrees. Lightly oil a 9 x 13-inch glass or ceramic baking dish. Mix the cheeses together and set a third of the cheese aside. Spread 1/4 cup salsa over the bottom and sides of the baking dish. Working with one tortilla at a time, layer the cheese, vegetables, corn, and turkey down the middle length of a tortilla. Holding the sides of the tortilla up with your pinkies to prevent the filling from falling out, roll the tortilla tightly over the stuffing and transfer to the prepared baking dish, seam side down.

**4.** Do this with the remaining tortillas until all four burritos are laid side-by-side in the baking dish. Top with the remaining 1 3/4 cups salsa and cheeses. At this point, the burritos can be covered with foil, wrapped tightly with plastic wrap, and frozen for up to 1 month before baking per the directions below.

**5.** Transfer the baking dish to the oven and bake until the cheese browns in spots and the burritos are heated through, about 40 minutes. Let rest for 10 minutes before serving.

**6.** To bake from frozen, preheat the oven to 350 degrees. Remove the baking dish of burritos from the freezer and unwrap (leaving the foil in place). Bake for 40 minutes, remove the foil, and bake until the cheese browns in spots and the burritos are heated through, another 20 to 40 minutes.

**7.** To serve, toss the remaining shredded cabbage and lime juice together. Top each serving with the cabbage mixture.

# TURKEY TORTILLA SOUP

I like to serve tortilla soup just like you would tacos, with plenty of tableside garnishes. This allows even the pickiest of eaters to customize according to their particular tastes. This book is chock-full of condiments and pantry staples that would be fabulous additions to this soup, which comes together quickly from leftover **OLD BAY ROASTED TURKEY BREAST, PLUS TURKEY STOCK** (page 138). I recommend setting up a restaurant-worthy garnish bar with **ESCABECHE** (page 86), **POBLANO RELISH** (page 89), **QUICK PICKLED RED ONIONS** (page 84), **RED FRESNO SRIRACHA** (page 67), and **TOMATILLO AVOCADO SALSA VERDE** (page 77).

**MAKES 2 QUARTS, SERVES 6 TO 8**

1 1/4 pounds Roma tomatoes, cored and halved lengthwise (about 7)
1 white onion, peeled and quartered through the poles, leaving root intact so the layers remain connected
2 serrano peppers
4 medium cloves garlic, unpeeled
2 tablespoons expeller-pressed safflower oil, divided
1 1/2 teaspoons kosher salt, divided
Pinch of black pepper
1 dried ancho chile pepper, stem removed and roughly chopped
2 quarts Turkey Stock (page 140)
1 tablespoon red wine vinegar
1 pound turkey meat from Old Bay Roasted Turkey Breast (page 138), skin removed and reserved, meat shredded into bite-size pieces
Crispy Tortilla Strips (recipe follows)

**POTENTIAL GARNISHES (A FEW TABLESPOONS PER SERVING):**
diced avocado, chopped fresh cilantro, crumbled cheese (like cotija), and diced onion

1. Preheat the oven to 425 degrees.

2. In a large bowl, toss together the tomatoes, onion, serrano peppers, garlic, 1 tablespoon of the oil, 1/2 teaspoon of the salt, and pepper and spread evenly on a baking sheet. Roast until charred in spots, 10 to 15 minutes. Remove from the heat and set aside.

3. Meanwhile, in a stockpot, soak the ancho chile pepper in the turkey stock until pliable, about 20 minutes.

**4.** When the vegetables are cool enough to handle, peel the garlic and stem the serrano peppers. Add all of the vegetables, remaining 1 teaspoon salt, and vinegar to the stockpot. Bring to a boil over high heat, reduce the heat to medium, and simmer for 10 minutes.

**5.** While the soup simmers, roughly chop the turkey skin. In a medium skillet over low heat, heat the remaining 1 tablespoon oil, add the chopped skin, and cook until fully rendered, about 5 minutes. Then add the skin and rendered oil to the soup.

**6.** Using an immersion blender, puree the soup until mostly smooth. Alternatively, cool the soup to room temperature before pulsing or blending in a food processor or standing blender.

**7.** To serve, add the turkey, return to a boil, then remove from the heat. Serve, passing the tortilla strips and garnishes at the table.

---

### PRO TIP

Use the turkey skin like bacon to add depth of flavor to this soup.

---

## CRISPY TORTILLA STRIPS

**MAKES ABOUT 2 CUPS**

1 cup expeller-pressed safflower oil
8 (5-inch) corn tortillas, cut into strips
Pinch of kosher salt

*Also a great topping for scrambled eggs!*

In a saucepan over medium heat, heat the oil until shimmering, 1 to 2 minutes. Add half of the tortilla strips and fry until crisp and the bubbling ceases, 2 to 3 minutes. Use a slotted or mesh spoon to remove the tortilla strips to a paper towel–lined baking sheet. Repeat with the remaining tortilla strips. Toss the finished crispy tortilla strips with salt.

Turkey

MAXIMUS/MINIMUS
GRILLED CHICKEN
THIGHS

Chicken

# PAN-ROASTED CHICKEN BREASTS, PLUS STOCK

*(As seen on page 16)* I'm no big fan of your average chicken breast—thighs are usually juicier and more flavorful—but if treated properly, as here, breast meat can really shine. This recipe yields chicken for several meals. It is the parent recipe for **HEARTY CHICKEN SOUP** (page 152) and **CHICKEN SALAD VINDALOO** (page 151). Prepared as is, these chicken breasts pair nicely with **ANCHO ROASTED CARROTS** (page 197).

**SERVES 10**

10 bone-in, skin-on chicken breast halves
2 tablespoons expeller-pressed safflower oil, divided
1 tablespoon kosher salt
1/2 teaspoon black pepper
1 teaspoon dried oregano
1/2 teaspoon granulated garlic
1/2 teaspoon ground cumin
1/2 teaspoon paprika

**1.** With skin side facing up, use the tip of your knife and a series of lengthwise shallow cuts to gently remove each breast from either side of the central breastbone and back ribs. Set the breasts aside in a large bowl. Set the bones aside for making the Chicken Stock (recipe follows).

**2.** Thoroughly mix the chicken with 1 tablespoon of the oil and the salt, pepper, and spices until evenly coated. Cover and place in the refrigerator for 1 to 24 hours (longer is better).

**3.** Preheat the oven to 375 degrees.

**4.** In a large, oven-safe skillet over high heat, heat the remaining 1 tablespoon oil until smoking. Add 5 breasts skin side down and cook until brown, 5 to 7 minutes. Turn the breasts over and immediately transfer the skillet to the oven and bake until tender and no longer pink, 15 to 20 minutes, depending on the thickness of the breasts. Repeat with the second batch.

## PRO TIP

Buy whole chicken breasts and take them off the bone yourself, so that you can use the bones for stock (see accompanying recipe).

# CHICKEN STOCK

**MAKES ABOUT 2 QUARTS**

Chicken bones from 10 chicken breast halves
Pinch of salt and black pepper
10 cups water

1. Preheat the oven to 425 degrees.

2. Cut the bones of each whole breast into quarters using kitchen shears. In a large bowl, toss the bones with the salt and pepper. Spread the bones on a baking sheet and roast until deeply browned, 30 to 35 minutes.

3. Remove the bones from the oven and transfer to a stockpot, covering with the water. Bring to a boil, reduce the heat to medium-low, and simmer until the liquid reduces by 20 percent, about 1 hour.

4. Using a mesh strainer, strain, cool, and store until ready to use, in the refrigerator for up to 1 week or the freezer for up to 3 months.

# CHICKEN SALAD VINDALOO

This is my more contemporary take on classic curried chicken salad. Vindaloo is a spicier type of curry powder and creates a great dressing when mixed with tangy Greek yogurt. If you can't find vindaloo, any high-quality curry powder will work. This salad is a perfect way to turn left-over **PAN-ROASTED CHICKEN BREASTS** (page 148) into a flavorful lunch.

**SERVES 4 TO 6**

4 cooked chicken breast halves (from Pan-Roasted Chicken Breasts, page 148)
2 tablespoons chopped fresh tarragon leaves
3/4 teaspoon kosher salt
1/2 cup plain whole milk Greek yogurt
1/3 cup water
2 tablespoons vindaloo curry powder
4 teaspoons red wine vinegar
1/2 cup shelled pistachios
1 cup halved seedless grapes
2 celery ribs, diced (about 1 cup)
1 small head frisée, separated into leaves
1 small head radicchio, separated into leaves
1/4 cup Quick Pickled Red Onions (page 84)

1. Remove the chicken skin and set aside if making Chicken Chicharron (see note). Using forks or your fingers, shred the meat into bite-size pieces.

2. Mix the tarragon, salt, yogurt, water, vindaloo, and vinegar together in a bowl. Using the side of a large chef's knife, lightly smash the pistachios (alternatively, coarsely chop). Add the pistachios, chicken, grapes, and celery to the yogurt mixture, and stir to combine. Store covered in the refrigerator until ready to serve, up to 3 days.

3. To serve, place the chicken salad on a bed of frisée and radicchio leaves and top with Quick Pickled Red Onions and Chicken Chicharron (optional, see note).

**NOTE:**
To make Chicken Chicharron, preheat 1 teaspoon expeller-pressed safflower oil in a skillet until shimmering. Add the chicken skin and cook, stirring occasionally, until fully rendered and browned, 2 to 5 minutes. Remove and set aside on a paper towel–lined plate.

*lower the heat toward the end to prevent burning*

Chicken

151

# HEARTY CHICKEN SOUP

*(As seen on page 2)* Here's a great way to put together a quick meal from leftover **PAN-ROASTED CHICKEN BREASTS, PLUS STOCK** (page 148). The potatoes, cooked in the stock and then pureed, add body to the broth. Chicken skin is used much like bacon in this recipe, to add a savory richness to this hearty soup.

**SERVES 4 TO 6**

2 tablespoons expeller-pressed safflower oil, divided
3 medium cloves garlic, minced
1/4 teaspoon red pepper flakes
1 1/2 cups diced Yukon gold potatoes (about 7 ounces)
1 recipe Chicken Stock (page 149)
2 cooked chicken breast halves (from Pan-Roasted Chicken Breasts, page 148), skin removed and reserved, meat shredded into bite-size pieces
2 teaspoons kosher salt
2 carrots, sliced (about 1 1/2 cups)
1 yellow onion, diced (about 1 cup)
2 celery ribs, sliced (about 1 cup)
1 (12-ounce) can diced tomatoes, drained
1 tablespoon roughly chopped fresh thyme leaves
1 ear corn, kernels cut from cob (about 1 cup)

1. In a Dutch oven over low heat, heat 1 tablespoon of the oil until shimmering, 1 to 2 minutes. Add the garlic and red pepper flakes and cook until fragrant, 1 minute. Add the potatoes and chicken stock and increase the heat to high. Bring to a boil, reduce the heat to low, and simmer until the potatoes break apart upon touch, 15 minutes.

2. While the soup simmers, roughly chop the chicken skin. In a medium skillet over low heat, heat the remaining 1 tablespoon oil, add the chopped skin, and cook until fully rendered, about 5 minutes. Remove the soup from the heat.

3. Add the skin and rendered oil to the soup and, using an immersion blender, puree the mixture until no visible potato pieces remain. Alternatively, cool to room temperature, puree using a standing blender or food processor, and return the mixture to the Dutch oven.

4. Return the pot to medium heat, add the salt, carrots, onion, celery, tomatoes, and thyme, and cook until tender, 15 minutes. Add the chicken and corn and return to a simmer, cooking until warmed through. Serve immediately or cool and store in the refrigerator for up to 5 days or the freezer for up to 3 months.

# MAXIMUS/MINIMUS GRILLED CHICKEN THIGHS

*(As seen on page 146-147)* Chicken thighs are naturally richer and more flavorful than chicken breasts, and their higher fat content makes them more forgiving and less likely to dry out under high-heat grilling. We serve these chicken thighs as a sandwich on a burger bun at Maximus/Minimus, my food truck in Seattle. Even though the truck is shaped like a pig and a pulled pork sandwich is the headliner, this sandwich is my go-to order. If you have the time, mix the marinade together and set it aside for half an hour to allow the cumin and fennel seeds to soften before adding the chicken. Because the marinade includes lime juice, do not leave the raw chicken in it for longer than specified in step 2 or the acidity will break down the proteins in the meat and make the chicken mushy and mealy.

**SERVES 8 TO 10**

3/4 cup lime juice
1/2 cup (plus 2 tablespoons, if using stove-top cooking method)
   expeller-pressed safflower oil
2 teaspoons granulated garlic
2 tablespoons dried oregano
2 tablespoons kosher salt
4 teaspoons chili powder
2 teaspoons black pepper
1 teaspoon cumin seed
1/2 teaspoon fennel seed
5 pounds boneless, skinless chicken thighs

1. To make the marinade, in a large bowl, whisk together the lime juice, 1/2 cup oil, garlic, and spices. Add the chicken and toss to coat evenly. Set aside at room temperature for 30 minutes.

2. To grill, turn all burners to high, cover, and heat the grill until hot, about 15 minutes. Clean and oil the cooking grate. Place the chicken on the grill, smooth side down, and cook until the chicken is charred in spots on the first side, about 5 minutes. Flip the chicken and cook until browned on the second side and the chicken is tender and no longer pink, about 5 minutes. Transfer the chicken to a plate and let rest for 5 minutes before serving.

3. To cook on the stove top, heat 2 tablespoons expeller-pressed safflower oil in a large skillet over high heat until smoking, 2 to 3 minutes. Add the chicken thighs, smooth side down, and cook without moving until the bottom side is well charred, about 4 minutes. Flip the chicken, reduce the heat to low, and cook until the chicken is tender and no longer pink, about 10 minutes.

# BEER-BRINED CHICKEN WINGS
# WITH RED FRESNO SRIRACHA

I developed this recipe as part of a collaboration between Samuel Adams and Beecher's. While any lager will do for use in these wings, I really do prefer their Boston Lager. This recipe delivers the same punchy flavor and juicy, crisp texture as your favorite bar wings, without the deep-frying and additive-laden sauces they typically rely upon. The cornstarch helps the wings brown and gives the sauce something to cling to.

**SERVES 6 TO 12**

4 (12-ounce) cans beer, preferably lager
6 tablespoons kosher salt
3 tablespoons brown sugar
3 to 4 pounds chicken wings, separated into drumettes with tips discarded
1 tablespoon cornstarch
1/2 cup Red Fresno Sriracha (page 67)

**1.** To make the brine, in a large saucepan, bring the beer, salt, and sugar to a simmer. Watch closely when the beer nears a boil; it can foam up and over the edge of the pan. Use a spoon to stir the bubbles down. Simmer for 3 to 4 minutes. Remove from the heat, pour into a large bowl (large enough to hold the chicken wings and liquid), and cool. The brine can be made a day ahead and refrigerated. (Do not add the chicken to the hot brine.)

**2.** Combine the brine and the chicken in the large bowl and refrigerate for 1 to 2 hours, but not longer. Remove the chicken, rinse, and pat dry with paper towels. (Brined and dried wings can be stored in the refrigerator for up to 24 hours.)

**3.** Preheat the oven to 500 degrees.

**4.** In a large bowl, toss the chicken wings with the cornstarch. Spread the chicken wings on a lightly oiled baking sheet. Bake until well browned and cooked through, 15 to 20 minutes, flipping the wings halfway through the cooking time.

**5.** In a clean, large bowl, toss the cooked wings with the Red Fresno Sriracha and return to the baking sheet, scraping any residual sauce from the bowl onto the wings. Continue baking for 3 to 5 minutes or until the optional cheese is bubbling. Let the wings cool for a few minutes on the baking sheet before serving.

For extra incredible-ness top the wings with cheese before the last time in the oven

Seafood

# WHITE FISH SALAD

*This is a great recipe. Try it!*

This fish salad is a great make-ahead recipe for a hot summer day. It's heavy on vegetables, and can easily work on its own as an entrée. When buying the fish for this salad, ask your fishmonger for the freshest option with thin skin and firm, but not oily, flesh. You'll find that the skin holds the fish together when you're preparing this dish—plus, it adds great flavor. I like to use branzino or red snapper, but trout, porgy, orata, black cod, and sea bream will also work well. Make sure that the fish is free of all bones. A good fishmonger will debone it for you, if asked; otherwise, when cutting the fish into cubes, either tweezer them out individually or simply discard the pin bone section that runs down the center of each fillet.

**SERVES 4**

1 1/2 pounds (ideally skin-on) small white fish fillets,
    cut into roughly 1 1/2-inch cubes
1 tablespoon chopped fresh oregano
1 teaspoon kosher salt
1/4 teaspoon black pepper
1/4 cup plus 2 tablespoons expeller-pressed safflower oil, divided
4 ounces mini sweet peppers (see note page 161),
    roughly chopped on the bias into 1-inch pieces (about 1 cup)
1/2 sweet onion, chopped (about 3/4 cup)
1 medium clove garlic, peeled and chopped
1/2 cup chopped fresh dill
1/2 fennel bulb, thinly shaved lengthwise and
    cut crosswise into 1-inch strips
1/4 cup chopped and pitted kalamata olives (about 12 olives)
4 Campari tomatoes (or other small tomatoes), sliced into 1/8-inch rounds
2 tablespoons capers, drained
1 teaspoon red pepper flakes
1/2 cup extra-virgin olive oil
1 lemon, juiced (2 to 3 tablespoons juice)

**1.** Sprinkle the fish fillet cubes with the oregano, salt, and pepper. In a large skillet over medium-high heat, heat 1/4 cup of the safflower oil until shimmering. Working in 3 to 5 batches to prevent crowding, add the fish skin side down and cook until the skin is golden and the flesh just turns opaque, 2 to 3 minutes, turning the thicker pieces if necessary to achieve proper doneness without burning the skin. Using tongs or  >>

a slotted spoon, transfer the done pieces of fish to a large bowl, discarding the cooking oil but not washing the skillet.

**2.** Add the remaining 2 tablespoons safflower oil to the skillet and set to high heat until the oil is smoking. Add the peppers and onion. Stir the mixture once to coat with the oil, then let cook without stirring until the vegetables begin to brown, about 3 minutes. Toss the vegetables and continue browning for 2 more minutes. Turn off the heat, add the garlic, and cook, stirring, until aromatic, about 1 minute. Transfer the vegetables to the large bowl with the fish and set aside to cool to room temperature.

**3.** Add the remaining ingredients to the bowl and gently toss to combine, without breaking the pieces of fish. Eat immediately or cover and keep in the refrigerator for up to 24 hours, removing from refrigeration 30 to 60 minutes before serving.

**NOTE:**
If you can't find mini sweet peppers, substitute a combination of yellow, red, and orange bell peppers, cut into 1- to 2-inch pieces.

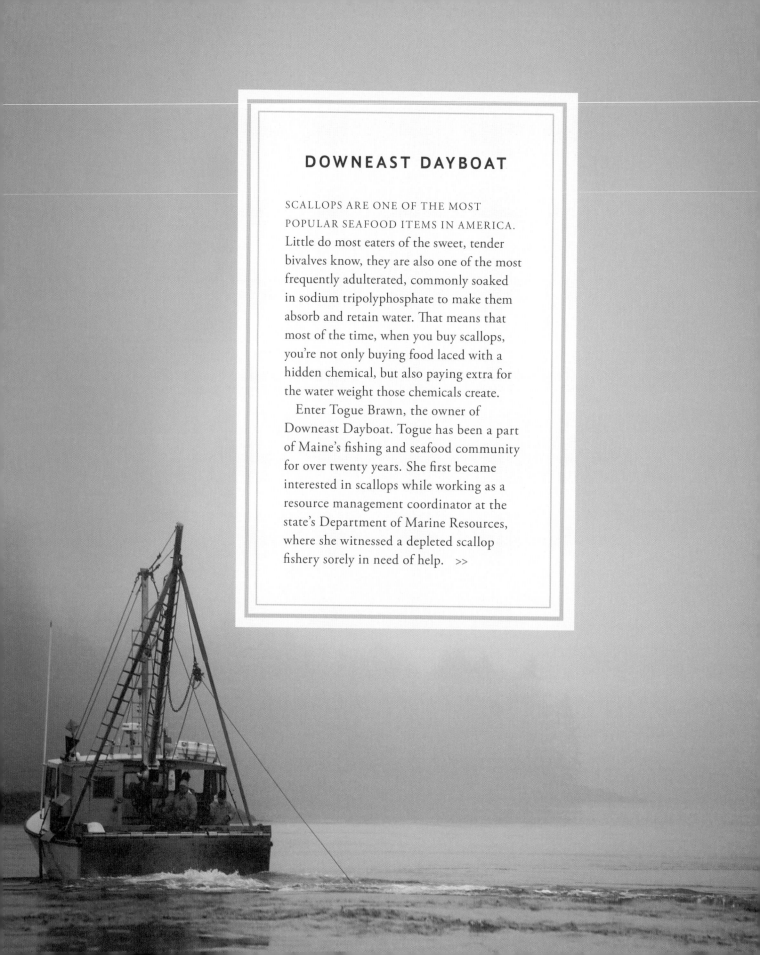

## DOWNEAST DAYBOAT

SCALLOPS ARE ONE OF THE MOST POPULAR SEAFOOD ITEMS IN AMERICA. Little do most eaters of the sweet, tender bivalves know, they are also one of the most frequently adulterated, commonly soaked in sodium tripolyphosphate to make them absorb and retain water. That means that most of the time, when you buy scallops, you're not only buying food laced with a hidden chemical, but also paying extra for the water weight those chemicals create.

Enter Togue Brawn, the owner of Downeast Dayboat. Togue has been a part of Maine's fishing and seafood community for over twenty years. She first became interested in scallops while working as a resource management coordinator at the state's Department of Marine Resources, where she witnessed a depleted scallop fishery sorely in need of help.  >>

SCALLOP CRUDO

She worked with the state's fishermen to reduce the length of their season, decrease the daily catch limits, and close off areas of the coast as conservation areas. "We put in laws that involved short-term pain for long-term gain," Togue said. "Now we've got a thriving resource."

Togue started her company, Downeast Dayboat, in 2011, after realizing that small fishermen bringing in pristine, ultra-fresh scallops were getting paid the same price, or even less, than commodity operations coming in with thousands of pounds of days-old mollusks. Her company connects delicious, 100 percent pure Maine scallops directly with the consumers, stores, and restaurants that appreciate a great product and are willing to pay extra for it.

To understand the real value of the scallops that Togue sells, you have to understand what she's competing against. About 95 percent of the scallops caught in the U.S. come from so-called "trip boats": outfits that stay out on the water for days at a time, as opposed to day boats, which go out and come back within one day. Trip boats stay at sea for a week at a time, on average. As the scallops are caught, they're stored in cloth bags buried in ice. Over the course of the trip, that ice melts and the bivalves absorb the fresh water. Scallops are naturally 76 to 78 percent water; when they come off trip boats, they often clock in at over 80 percent.

Trip boats offload thousands of pounds of old, waterlogged scallops at a time, which get funneled into a distribution chain that usually includes many steps, over the course of many days, on their way to the end consumer. Often, the scallops get soaked in sodium tripolyphosphate solutions along the way, causing them to absorb yet more water and pump up their price.

Togue's system operates very differently. She works directly with small boat fishermen in Maine—a state that has a "day boat only" policy when it comes to scallop fishing, meaning the big trip boats are prohibited from operating in state waters. Togue's fishermen measure their voyages in hours, not days. Depending on where they fish, they can bring in 90, 135, or 200 pounds per trip. Her scallops never touch fresh water, let alone chemicals.

"I always knew Maine scallops were better, but to be honest I didn't realize just how much better they were until I started bringing them to New York City and shipping them around the country," Togue said. "And I didn't realize just how pervasive soaking was until I started hearing people tell me they'd never tried a scallop like mine."

As a consumer, trying to figure out whether the scallops you're buying are fresh and additive-free can be difficult and frustrating. There is little in the way of regulation governing how scallops are labeled, and what regulation there is isn't uniformly enforced; thank the powerful commercial scallop industry and its lobbyists for that. Technically, scallops with a moisture content above 82 percent cannot legally be labeled as "dry-packed"—a term that means the scallops weren't treated with phosphates—but in practice, supermarkets are full of fraudulent products. "You're at the mercy of the guy who you're buying from, and he's at the mercy of the guy he bought from," Togue said.

The term "diver scallops" is another common subject of fraud. The designation refers to scallops hand-harvested by divers in a minimally invasive fashion, but it's widely misused. Togue suggests looking for scallops labeled "day boat," without paying too much attention to the "diver" terminology.

Before you buy scallops, ask where they came from. Since Maine only allows day boats in state waters, you can be sure that scallops caught there haven't been sitting in ice on a ship for a week.

Scallops treated with phosphates often look and taste slightly different than additive-free ones. There's often a slight metallic taste to a scallop that's been soaked in phosphates. These chemicals also tend to bleach the color of the seafood, so look for specimens with a nice pink blush to them (although it's possible for fresh scallops to be very pale in color, too).

But the best way to ensure that you're getting good-quality scallops is to buy them from a trusted source: ideally, directly from a fisherman, right off the boat. If you can't source your scallops this way, then try mail-ordering them from a reputable dealer. Downeast Dayboat, Sea to Table, and Browne Trading Company are all excellent choices. The more steps there are in the chain between ocean and eater, the older the scallops are, and the greater the chances that they were adulterated along the way.

> Before you buy scallops, ask where they came from. Since Maine only allows day boats in state waters, you can be sure that scallops caught there haven't been sitting in ice on a ship for a week.

# SCALLOP CRUDO

*(As seen on page 163)* For this crudo dish, as with any raw preparation, using sashimi-grade sea scallops is a must (ask your fishmonger if you're not certain about the grade of the scallops on offer). Instead of using regular old kosher salt, I like to finish the dish with black lava salt, but a smoked salt or pink salt would also do the trick.

**SERVES 4
AS AN
APPETIZER**

3/4 cup plus 2 teaspoons expeller-pressed safflower oil, divided
1/2 cup sliced red Fresno chiles (about 2 small chiles)
1/2 cup sliced jalapeño pepper (about 1 pepper)
1/4 cup chopped red onion
1/2 cup mashed avocado (about 1/2 large avocado or 1 small)
1/4 teaspoon Old Bay Seasoning
1/2 teaspoon orange zest, plus extra for garnish
8 sprigs cilantro
2 tablespoons orange juice
4 sea scallops, side muscle removed, rinsed and patted dry (about 5 ounces)
Hawaiian black lava sea salt, to taste

**1.** In a large skillet over high heat, heat 1/4 cup of the oil until smoking, about 1 minute. Add the chiles, jalapeño, and onion, and stir to fully coat them in oil and create one layer in the pan. Let cook for 45 seconds or until the pepper and chile are just starting to brown. Remove from the heat and add another 1/2 cup oil to the skillet. Stir and transfer the oil and pepper mixture to a medium bowl to let cool. (This oil mixture can be refrigerated in an airtight container for up to 5 days.)

**2.** In a small bowl, combine the avocado, Old Bay Seasoning, 1/2 teaspoon orange zest, and remaining 2 teaspoons oil. In a separate, small bowl, toss the cilantro with the orange juice. Prepare the scallops by slicing each scallop crosswise into 4 thin slices.

**3.** To plate, for each serving, spread 2 table-spoons of the avocado mixture in a straight line, about 2 inches wide, down the center of a small plate. Spread about 1 tablespoon of the onion from the oil down the line of avocado. Arrange 4 scallop slices on top of the onion. Top each scallop slice with 4 alternating slices of red Fresno chile and jalapeno pepper from the oil (2 slices of each). For more heat, add more slices of chiles and jalapeños. Top with a drizzle of the infused oil, sprinkle of salt, and orange zest, and two sprigs of cilantro. For a little extra flair, add 4 to 5 drops of infused oil in a line down the side of the avocado.

**4.** Repeat the plating steps for a total of 4 small dishes. Serve immediately.

# PAN-SEARED SCALLOPS WITH TARRAGON CORN

This is a perfect midsummer dish, when fresh corn and tomatoes are abundant. If you're in the mood for bolder flavor, add a little zip with **POBLANO RELISH** (page 89).

**SERVES 6**

18 sea scallops, side muscle removed, rinsed and patted dry
1 1/2 teaspoons kosher salt, divided, plus more to taste
1/2 teaspoon black pepper, divided, plus more to taste
3 tablespoons unsalted butter
1 large shallot, diced (about 1/2 cup)
3 ears corn, kernels cut from cob (about 2 cups kernels)
1/2 yellow bell pepper, diced
20 cherry tomatoes, halved
2 1/4 teaspoons chopped fresh tarragon
2 tablespoons white wine
1/2 cup heavy cream

1. In a large bowl, combine the scallops with 1/2 teaspoon salt and 1/4 teaspoon black pepper. In a large skillet over medium-high heat, melt the butter and cook until just browned. Place the scallops in the skillet, making sure they are not touching, and let cook for 3 1/2 minutes until they are browned and crispy, but not burned. Flip the scallops and let cook for 1 more minute until they are cooked through with the center of the scallop slightly translucent. Transfer the scallops to a clean bowl.

2. To the same skillet over medium-high heat, add the shallots and stir. The shallots should slightly deglaze the pan, about 30 seconds. Add the corn and bell pepper and continue stirring and cooking for another 30 seconds. Add the tomatoes, tarragon, and wine, and cook while stirring for 1 minute.

3. Add the cream, stir until it is heated through, and turn off the heat. Mix in the remaining 1 teaspoon salt and remaining 1/4 teaspoon black pepper, adding more to taste as needed.

4. From the reserved bowl of cooked scallops, pour the scallop juices back into the skillet and stir until the corn mixture is well combined.

5. Serve immediately, dividing the corn mixture among 6 dishes and topping each with 3 scallops.

Seafood

# HALIBUT CEVICHE

This is a regular menu item at Bennett's restaurant on "Mexican Monday." The most important thing is to seek out the highest quality, wild-caught seafood that you can find, since ceviche is a raw fish preparation and flavor and quality matter more than ever. Ask your local fishmonger to point you in the right direction. I prefer my ceviche "medium-rare," with the interior of the fish still translucent and only the exterior turned opaque by the acid in the lime juice. This requires only 5 minutes of marinating time. I add seasoned rice vinegar and honey to the usual lime marinade to give it a rounder flavor. To make this ceviche truly outstanding, I like to serve **RED FRESNO SRIRACHA** (page 67) alongside or over the top of individual portions. Consider serving it with tortilla or plantain chips and diced avocado.

**SERVES 4 AS AN ENTRÉE OR 8 AS AN APPETIZER**

1 medium clove garlic
1 teaspoon kosher salt
1/4 jalapeño pepper, stemmed and seeded
3/4 cup lime juice
6 tablespoons seasoned rice vinegar
6 tablespoons extra-virgin olive oil
1 teaspoon honey
8 ounces halibut, diced into 1/2-inch pieces
1/2 English cucumber, diced into 1/4-inch pieces
1/4 sweet onion, shaved thin into 1-inch lengths
2 tablespoons chopped fresh cilantro

1. Using a food processor, blend the garlic, salt, jalapeño, lime juice, vinegar, oil, and honey until smooth. (This dressing can be made up to 4 hours ahead and stored in the refrigerator until ready to serve.)

2. Just before serving, in a large bowl, gently mix the halibut, cucumber, onion, and cilantro with the lime dressing. Let marinate for up to 5 minutes, until the surface of the fish is opaque but the interior is still translucent. Serve immediately.

I developed this recipe after a visit to Peru, the capital of ceviche. It's a great country with really incredible food...

# FENNEL AND RED ONION CRUSTED
# HALIBUT WITH AIOLI

The nicely brown, crispy crust is part of what makes this recipe really delicious. To give the crust time to brown, make sure you work with only the thickest part of the fish. Ask your local fishmonger for the head side of the fish. And if you can't find halibut, you can use salmon for this dish with great results.

**SERVES 6 TO 8**

1 fennel bulb, stalk trimmed and discarded, bulb diced (about 1 1/4 cups)
1 red onion, diced (about 1 1/4 cups)
3 tablespoons white vinegar
2 3/4 teaspoons kosher salt, divided
1 tablespoon unsalted butter
3/4 plus 1/8 teaspoon black pepper, divided
2 pounds 12 ounces halibut, skinned and cut into 6 to 8 portions
2 teaspoons The Butcher's Table Seasoning Blend (page 63)
2 teaspoons all-purpose flour
2 egg yolks
3/4 teaspoon lemon juice, plus more to taste
1 cup expeller-pressed safflower oil
2 tablespoons fresh dill
1/4 teaspoon lemon zest
1/4 teaspoon granulated garlic

**1.** In a medium bowl, mix the fennel and onion together. Set aside 1 1/2 cups of the mixture. To the remaining 1 cup in the bowl, add the vinegar and 1 teaspoon of the salt and stir. Refrigerate the mixture for 1 hour to pickle it. (The longer you marinate the mixture, the more brightly red the onions turn.)

**2.** While the onion and fennel is pickling, preheat the oven to 400 degrees. Line a baking sheet with parchment paper.

**3.** In a small skillet over medium-high heat, melt the butter. Add the reserved 1 1/2 cups fennel and onion mixture. Stir, sprinkle with 1 teaspoon salt and 1/4 teaspoon of the black pepper, and let sit for 1 minute. Stir and let cook for another 1 1/2 minutes, stirring occasionally. Remove from the heat and set aside.

**4.** Add the halibut to a medium-size bowl and sprinkle with The Butcher's Table Seasoning Blend, 1/2 teaspoon salt, and 1/8 teaspoon black pepper. Gently toss until each piece of halibut is thoroughly coated. Place the halibut on the parchment-lined baking sheet.

**5.** To the cooked fennel and onion mixture, add the flour and stir until thoroughly mixed. Equally distribute the mixture across the pieces of halibut, spreading it evenly and pressing it down to adhere.

**6.** Bake the halibut in the oven for 15 to 25 minutes, depending on the thickness of your fish. Turn the broiler on to high and broil until the halibut topping is lightly browned, making sure not to overcook the fish.

**7.** While the halibut is baking, make the aioli. Place the egg yolks, lemon juice,

and remaining 1/4 teaspoon salt in a food processor and process to combine, scraping down the sides and bottom of the bowl as necessary. With the processor running, very slowly stream in the first 2 to 4 tablespoons of oil. If done correctly, the oil and other ingredients should create an emulsion that appears thicker. Allow the processor to run for 1 minute before slowly streaming in the remaining oil, processing until fully combined and thickened like mayonnaise.

**8.** Add the dill, remaining 1/2 teaspoon black pepper, lemon zest, and garlic, and pulse to combine. Drain the pickled fennel and onion mixture. Add the mixture to the food processor and pulse until just combined. (The aioli can be stored in an airtight container in the refrigerator for up to 1 week.)

**9.** Serve the halibut warm alongside the aioli.

*Do this at the end of cooking if necessary to crisp the coating.*

Grains

# SMOKY GRITS

Grits are the quintessential Southern starch, served at all times of day alongside everything from eggs to braised dishes. Consider serving this recipe with **BRAISED PORK SHOULDER** (page 131) and **WILTED COLLARD GREENS** (page 213) for the ultimate nod to Southern cuisine.

**SERVES 4 TO 6
AS A SIDE DISH**

2 cups Chicken Stock (page 149)

2 1/2 cups water

1 1/2 cups grits

1 1/2 teaspoons kosher salt

6 ounces Beecher's Smoked Flagship cheese (page 66 for alternate), grated (about 1 1/2 cups)

3 tablespoons unsalted butter

1/2 teaspoon black pepper

**1.** In a large pot, bring the stock and water to a boil over high heat. Whisk in the grits and salt and return to a boil. Reduce the heat to medium-low and stir constantly until thickened, about 5 minutes.

**2.** Remove the grits from the heat and whisk in the cheese, butter, and pepper. Serve immediately.

---

### PRO TIP

Leftover grits can be cooled and stored in the refrigerator for a few days. They will cool into a solid block that can be sliced and pan-fried. I like to serve this, instead of toast, topped with fried eggs for breakfast.

# POLENTA VERDURE (I ♡ polenta)

Layers of polenta, cheese, and vegetables come together in this impressive vegetarian main course. This recipe makes use of leftover roasted vegetables (pages 194–197) and **SPICY OVEN-DRIED TOMATO SAUCE** (page 81). With these ingredients already made, dinner can be assembled in 10 minutes and on the table in an hour. If you prefer to make this dish ahead, it can be baked, cooled, and stored in the refrigerator for up to 5 days. Individual servings can be reheated and then topped with warmed tomato sauce and basil dressed with lemon juice.

**SERVES 6 TO 8**

1 1/2 cups polenta
1 teaspoon plus a pinch of kosher salt, divided
1/2 teaspoon black pepper
4 1/2 cups water
12 ounces Beecher's Flagship cheese (page 66 for alternate),
   grated (about 3 cups), divided
1 1/2 pounds roasted vegetables (pages 194–197; about 4 cups)
1 cup basil leaves, chopped
1/2 teaspoon lemon juice
2 cups Spicy Oven-Dried Tomato Sauce (page 81), warmed

1. Preheat the oven to 350 degrees. Lightly oil a 9 x 13-inch glass or ceramic baking dish.

2. In a large saucepan over medium-high heat, combine the polenta, 1 teaspoon of the salt, and the pepper with the water, and bring to a boil. Reduce the heat to medium-low and simmer, stirring frequently, until thickened, 5 minutes. Remove from the heat, stir in 3 ounces of the cheese, and pour half of the polenta mixture into the baking dish. Smooth the surface into an even layer and top with the roasted vegetables, followed by another 6 ounces of cheese.

3. Dollop the remaining half of the polenta mixture over the cheese and spread into an even layer. Top with the remaining 3 ounces cheese. Bake until bubbling and the dish is beginning to brown around the edges, 30 minutes. Let cool for 10 minutes.

4. While the polenta cools, toss together the basil, lemon juice, and the remaining pinch of salt in a small bowl.

5. To serve, top portions of the polenta with the warmed tomato sauce and the basil mixture.

# BREAD ALONE

DAN LEADER KNOWS THAT REAL BREAD, MADE THE WAY IT HAS BEEN FOR CENTURIES, CONSISTS OF VERY FEW INGREDIENTS: flour, water, salt, and sometimes yeast. That's it. Dan started Bread Alone bakery in October 1983. Inspired by the bakeries he visited in France, and the classic back-to-the-land text *Living the Good Life* by Scott and Helen Nearing, he left his job as a chef in New York City and moved his family up to the Hudson Valley. He built a wood-fire brick oven. He started Bread Alone. >>

Thirty-two years later, Dan and his team make 50 tons of bread a week, which they sell through grocery stores, farmers' markets, and at their own shops. Sandwich loaves, French-style sourdoughs, baguettes, challahs, and ciabattas are just a few of the many styles of bread that emerge from the Bread Alone ovens. Most are organic. Bread Alone is highly unusual among commercial bakeries, even organic ones, in that not a single loaf in its lineup contains food additives: no dough conditioners, emulsifiers, texturing agents, trans fats, preservatives, or sugars.

Pick up a loaf of conventional sandwich bread—the soft, pre-sliced kind sold wrapped in plastic in supermarkets—and you'll see just how radically different his approach is. Here's one example, from an Arnold brand bread being billed as "12 Grain":

WHOLE WHEAT FLOUR, UNBLEACHED ENRICHED WHEAT FLOUR [FLOUR, MALTED BARLEY FLOUR, REDUCED IRON, NIACIN, THIAMIN MONONITRATE (VITAMIN B1), RIBOFLAVIN (VITAMIN B2), FOLIC ACID], WATER, SUGAR, SUNFLOWER SEEDS, WHEAT GLUTEN, WHEAT, RYE, CELLULOSE FIBER, OATS, YEAST, SOYBEAN OIL, GROUND CORN, SALT, MOLASSES, BUCKWHEAT, BROWN RICE, CALCIUM PROPIONATE (PRESERVATIVE), MONOGLYCERIDES, TRITICALE, BARLEY, FLAXSEED, MILLET, CALCIUM SULFATE, DATEM, GRAIN VINEGAR, CALCIUM CARBONATE, CITRIC ACID, SOY LECITHIN, NUTS [WALNUTS AND/OR HAZELNUTS (FILBERTS) AND/OR ALMONDS], WHEY, SOY FLOUR, NONFAT MILK.

Cellulose fiber? Soy lecithin? Calcium carbonate? Soybean oil? There are at least sixteen ingredients on this label that have no business being in bread, additives aimed at making it cheap to produce and fluffier, softer, and longer lasting than bread has any business being.

Dan's techniques are drawn from traditional European practices, making breads in very small batches and allowing them long, slow fermentation periods to develop flavor and plenty of pillowy volume (without the addition of lots of extra gluten or industrial proofing agents). Bread Alone is best known for its sourdoughs, which are made from just flour, water, salt, and sourdough culture—a fermenting mass of complex enzymes, acids, and bacteria. Some of their breads take as much as 30 to 35 hours to make, from start to finish.

Bread Alone has worked with organic ingredients since the very beginning. Dan says he went this direction in the early 1980s, well before it was fashionable to do so, because he "had a gut feeling it would be important." He wanted to do something simpler and cleaner than what was currently on the market.

The bread landscape has changed a lot since Dan went into business. Bread Alone is part of the first generation of organic bakeries, which started when there were few people growing and milling organic flour and just a small subset of the population appreciated what it meant. "Today, you've got multibillion-dollar companies controlling the organic food movement," Dan said. "It's amazing to see the progress, but also upsetting to see what it's turning into."

What troubles Dan today is the number of breads marketing themselves as "natural" or "organic" that, when it comes to additives, are just as toxic as conventional options. "When you think of 'bad' bread, you think of Pepperidge Farm and Wonder Bread," Dan said. "But if you go and buy Rudy's Organic Bread or Dave's Killer Bread or Vermont Bread, it's Certified Organic, but there's a whole list of preservatives in there."

For instance, commercial bakers add a preservative called calcium propionate to keep their bread from molding, which organic certification doesn't allow. But many so-called "organic" bakers add "cultured wheat starch," an ingredient that produces calcium propionate—effectively sneaking the chemical in underneath consumers' noses. This practice is outlawed in Europe, but an FDA loophole makes it perfectly legal in the U.S.

Today, even with a large and growing segment of America interested in eating pure food, education is still a huge challenge for Bread Alone; thanks to the ultra-processed foods that flood our grocery stores, most consumers now believe that bread should have a two-week shelf life. "Our bread doesn't contain any preservatives whatsoever, and they're comparing it to breads that don't mold after twenty-eight days," Dan said. "Our basic rule for bread is that it shouldn't stay fresher than chicken in your refrigerator."

Keep that in mind the next time you shop for bread. Real bread is just flour, water, salt, and (sometimes) yeast. It should be highly perishable, keeping for a maximum of a few days on your counter or in the refrigerator.

Bread Alone is highly unusual among commercial bakeries, even organic ones, in that not a single loaf in its lineup contains food additives. No dough conditioners, emulsifiers, texturing agents, trans fats, preservatives, or sugars.

# PANZANELLA SALAD

This salad is great alongside grilled steak during tomato season. The dressing gets its complex tomato flavor from **OVEN-DRIED TOMATOES** (page 78), which have a heightened sweetness and depth of flavor compared to raw ones. I usually like to use heirloom tomatoes of various colors for this salad, but feel free to get creative with any variety at the peak of its season.

**SERVES 6**

2/3 cup extra-virgin olive oil, divided

2 teaspoons dried Italian herb blend

2 teaspoons kosher salt, divided

1/2 teaspoon black pepper

1 loaf olive bread, sliced into 1-inch cubes (about 1 pound)

1 1/2 ounces Beecher's Smoked Flagship cheese (page 66 for alternate), grated (about 1/3 cup)

3 ounces Oven-Dried Tomatoes (page 78; about 1/3 cup)

1/3 cup white balsamic vinegar

1/3 cup seasoned rice vinegar

1 teaspoon grainy mustard

1 teaspoon chopped fresh oregano leaves

1/2 teaspoon Tabasco

3 1/2 pounds tomatoes, cut into 1-inch cubes

2 cups torn basil leaves (1 large bunch)

1/2 cup thinly shaved sweet onion (about 1/2 onion)

1. Preheat the oven to 350 degrees.

2. In a large bowl, mix 1/3 cup of the oil, Italian herbs, 1 teaspoon of the salt, and pepper. Add the bread and sprinkle the cheese over the bread. Toss the mixture until evenly coated. Spread the bread mixture evenly on a baking sheet and bake until dried on the outside but a little soft in the center, about 15 minutes.

3. To a medium bowl, add the remaining 1/3 cup oil, Oven-Dried Tomatoes, balsamic and rice vinegars, mustard, oregano, and Tabasco. Using an immersion blender or a food processor, either blend or process the mixture until smooth.

4. In a large bowl, toss together the cubed tomatoes, basil, and onion with the bread cubes and dressing until well combined. Let rest for 10 minutes and then re-toss before serving.

NOTE:
The bread really matters
here. Look for a loaf with
an open, airy crumb that
contains big juicy pieces of
olives (black or green).

# CACIO E PEPE

Cacio e pepe derives its name and flavor from the inclusion of plenty of cheese and piquant freshly ground black pepper. This recipe combines those two ingredients plus green pepper-corns and arugula for a multidimensional pepper flavor. I like to use a mix of pasta shapes for visual and textural interest. Since different shapes often have different cooking times, be sure to read the package instructions and stagger their cooking times accordingly. Boiling the pasta in only 2 quarts of water yields a concentrated starchy liquid perfect for use as the base for the velvety cheese sauce.

*this technique can be used to thicken any sauce, even tomato and make it stick better to the pasta.*

**SERVES 4**

2 quarts water
2 teaspoons kosher salt, plus more to taste
8 ounces rigatoni
8 ounces fusilli
4 tablespoons unsalted butter
1 tablespoon loosely packed fresh oregano leaves
1 tablespoon coarsely ground green peppercorns
2 teaspoons coarsely ground black peppercorns
9 ounces Beecher's Flagship cheese (page 66 for alternate), grated (about 2 1/4 cups), divided
2 ounces baby arugula
4 to 8 tablespoons Nutty Cheesy Breadcrumbs (page 75)

**1.** In a large pot, bring the water and salt to a boil. Add the rigatoni and then, 1 minute later, add the fusilli. Cook the pasta until almost al dente, about 2 minutes less than the package instructions (it will finish cooking in the sauce). Strain the pasta, reserving the liquid. Set the pasta aside.

**2.** In a large wok (or skillet) over high heat, melt the butter. Add the oregano and green and black pepper and cook until fragrant, about 1 minute. Add 1 1/3 cups reserved pasta liquid and bring to a boil. Cook until reduced by one-fourth, about 2 minutes. Add the cooked pasta and toss until well coated and warmed through, about 3 minutes. Remove from the heat, add all but 1/3 cup cheese, and toss until the cheese is melted and the pasta is well coated. Stir in the arugula and serve immediately, topping with the remaining 1/3 cup cheese and the breadcrumbs.

# FARRO CAKES WITH BACON AND PARSLEY

We developed this recipe to serve as an accompaniment to meat at Bennett's restaurant. Molding farro into cake form adds a dimension and structure to the plate that a pile of loose grains simply cannot. I sometimes serve these cakes as a light supper with a small salad and sauces like **CHIMICHURRI** (page 73) or **RED FRESNO SRIRACHA** (page 67) and vegetable side dishes such as **RED CABBAGE PEPERONATA** (page 202) or **OVEN-DRIED TOMATOES** (page 78). This recipe easily doubles and leftovers reheat nicely in 15 minutes in a 350-degree oven.

**MAKES 5 CAKES**

1/2 pound farro
1/2 teaspoon kosher salt
1 cup water
1 cup Chicken Stock (page 149)
4 ounces bacon, roughly chopped
4 ounces Beecher's Flagship cheese (page 66 for alternate), grated (about 1 cup)
1/4 cup roughly chopped fresh flat-leaf parsley
2 tablespoons finely chopped Quick Pickled Red Onions (page 84)
1 1/2 teaspoons The Butcher's Table Seasoning Blend (page 63)
1/4 teaspoon black pepper
1 or 2 eggs, lightly beaten (see note)
2 tablespoons sherry vinegar

**1.** In a medium pot, bring the farro, salt, water, and stock to a boil over high heat. Reduce the heat to medium-high and cook at a simmer until the grains are tender and no unabsorbed liquid remains at the bottom of the pot, 25 to 30 minutes. If there is still liquid remaining when the grains are tender all the way through, turn the heat to high and cook, stirring frequently, until the excess liquid evaporates. Transfer the cooked grains to a large bowl to cool to room temperature.

**2.** In a medium skillet over medium heat, add the bacon and cook, stirring occasionally, until the bacon starts to brown, about 10 minutes. Reduce the heat to low and continue cooking until the bacon is fully rendered and no longer bubbling or foaming, 10 to 15 more minutes. Strain the bacon through a fine-mesh strainer set in a bowl, reserving the bacon fat. Chop the bacon pieces into a fine mince and add, along with 2 tablespoons of the bacon fat, to the large bowl with the cooling farro.

**3.** When the farro mixture is fully cooled to room temperature, add the cheese, parsley, onions, The Butcher's Table Seasoning Blend, black pepper, eggs, and vinegar, and mix thoroughly.

**4.** Preheat the oven to 425 degrees.

**5.** Use either a lightly greased ring mold or 1-cup dry measuring cup to shape the farro mixture into 3 1/2-inch diameter x 1-inch-thick densely packed cakes. If using a 1-cup measuring cup, use the back of a 1/2-cup measuring cup to pack the cakes down before tapping out onto a baking sheet. You should get 5 cakes.

**6.** Bake until nicely browned, 20 to 25 minutes.

**NOTE:**
Start with only one egg, but if the farro mixture fails to stick together when shaping, add the second egg.

---

**PRO TIP**

...........................................

The cakes are easier to shape when the cooked faro mixture has cooled to refrigerator temperature.

# RED QUINOA PILAF

*(As seen on page 172-173)* Red quinoa is a winner on all fronts. It's quick cooking, nutrient dense, visually appealing, and tasty when served warm, at room temperature, or cold from the refrigerator. This light, summery pilaf is loaded with vegetables and is equally appealing as a warm side dish or a packed lunch.

**SERVES 4 TO 6**

2 carrots, finely diced (about 1 cup)
1/2 teaspoon expeller-pressed safflower oil
1 1/2 teaspoons plus a pinch of kosher salt, divided
Pinch of black pepper
10 ounces dry quinoa (1 1/2 cups)
1 3/4 cups Chicken Stock (page 149)
1 medium tomato, diced (about 1 cup)
1 rib celery, diced (about 1/2 cup)
1/2 cup hazelnuts, lightly crushed or roughly chopped
1/2 red onion, minced (about 1/2 cup)
1/3 cup roughly chopped fresh flat-leaf parsley
2 teaspoons red wine vinegar

**1.** Preheat the oven to 450 degrees.

**2.** Toss the carrots with the oil and a pinch each of salt and pepper. Roast on a baking sheet until lightly browned and tender, 7 to 10 minutes.

**3.** Toast the quinoa in a dry, medium saucepan over medium-high heat, stirring frequently, until fragrant and popping, 5 to 7 minutes.

**4.** In a large saucepan over high heat, bring the stock, remaining 1 1/2 teaspoons salt, and quinoa to a boil. Reduce the heat to low and simmer until the quinoa is tender and all of the liquid has absorbed or evaporated, about 20 minutes. Remove the pan from the heat, cover, and let sit for 10 minutes.

**5.** In a large bowl, mix the cooked quinoa with the roasted carrots and remaining ingredients. Store in an airtight container in the refrigerator for up to 3 days.

# PAC 8 BROWN RICE SALAD

*(As seen on page 188)* This salad contains all the team colors in the original PAC 8 athletic conference, hence its name. It's a longtime favorite at my gourmet deli, Pasta & Co, where it's on the regular menu rotation. Make a big batch and use leftovers for packed lunches throughout the week. Boiling the brown rice like pasta, in plenty of salted water, keeps the grains from becoming gluey when chilled.

**SERVES 4**

3 quarts water

1 tablespoon plus 1 teaspoon kosher salt, divided

1 1/2 cups long-grain brown rice

12 ounces Maximus/Minimus Grilled Chicken Thighs (page 153),
   cut into 3/4-inch dice

1 bunch fresh cilantro, roughly chopped (about 2 cups)

1 1/2 cups Red Cabbage Peperonata (page 202),
   roughly chopped, plus 2 tablespoons liquid

1/2 cup slivered almonds

1/4 teaspoon black pepper

1 tablespoon lime juice

**1.** In a medium-size pot, bring the water and 1 tablespoon of the salt to a boil. Add the rice and cook until tender, 25 to 28 minutes. Drain well and spread evenly on a baking sheet to cool to room temperature before proceeding.

**2.** In a large bowl, combine the rice with the remaining 1 teaspoon salt and all of the remaining ingredients. Stir well to combine and serve.

**3.** This dish can be stored for up to 3 days in the refrigerator.

> ### PRO TIP
>
> ........................................
>
> To refresh this salad on day 2 or 3, drizzle it with olive oil and more lime juice.

PAC 8 BROWN RICE SALAD

## PASTA & CO

PASTA & CO HAS BEEN A SEATTLE INSTITUTION SINCE THE 1980S, a gourmet meal store where you can pick up soups, salads, appetizers, entrées, and desserts to heat and eat at home. Thai BBQ Chicken, Lentil Salad with Feta and Mint, Grilled Mushrooms, Coconut Layer Cake—Pasta & Co sells dishes that you'd be proud to put on your table, and which every Seattle host has probably passed off as his or her own at least once or twice. >>

When I bought the business in 2000 and got behind the kitchen doors, I was naive enough to be shocked and dismayed that some of the things that I assumed were being made from scratch were not. Don't get me wrong: compared to most food service operations, Pasta & Co was doing a really high-quality job. For the most part, they cooked their dishes exactly the way you would at home, using fresh whole vegetables and proteins and grains (as it turns out, that's pretty unusual in the restaurant world). Even so, there were additives lurking all over the place.

Take, for example, stock. I guess that I assumed that all restaurants made their stocks from scratch, simmering meats and vegetables in water to create fresh, flavorful broths. This is far from being the case. Almost none do! Making stock is expensive and time-consuming, and since it's always used merely as an ingredient in another recipe, rehydrating packaged bouillon cubes or concentrated, premade stock bases seems an obvious way to save on labor and ingredient costs. Pasta & Co used Knorr chicken stock and vegetable stock bases, and one or the other appeared in everything from soups to sauces to tortellini fillings.

Dehydrated stock bases are particularly gruesome in terms of the food additives they contain. Look at the back of a bouillon packet and the ingredients read like an industrial chemicals catalog; the first two ingredients are often salt and monosodium glutamate, followed by things like hydrolyzed corn protein, autolyzed yeast extract, disodium inosinate . . . the list goes on. It's a far cry from homemade chicken stock. As a matter of fact, "chicken" is often one of the last ingredients.

You could hardly blame me for thinking that restaurants relied purely on scratch cooking; they work hard to give off this impression to their diners. But the truth is that when you eat at a restaurant, you are entirely at the mercy of the chef and the decisions that he or she decides to make about your food. Unlike with packaged goods, where manufacturers are legally required to list all their ingredients, restaurants are under no obligation to tell you what chemicals or additives are in the food they serve. This goes for the little farm-to-table bistro down the street as well as massive chains like T.G.I. Fridays and Applebee's.

I knew that for the sake of my own conscience, we needed to make the food

> Unlike with packaged goods, where manufacturers are legally required to list all their ingredients, restaurants are under no obligation to tell you what chemicals or additives are in the food they serve.

at Pasta & Co additive-free—even if our customers didn't know or care about the difference (and in 2005, few people did). Luckily, in many aspects, Pasta & Co was already going above and beyond what 95 percent of restaurants would do. We made all our salad dressings in-house instead of buying the chemical-laden, premade stuff. We bought hormone-free milk. We've always used local bakeries for our breads, made without preservatives, dough conditioners, and the like. All of our desserts were made fresh, without artificial food colorings, frozen doughs, or mixes.

But we still had our work cut out for us. First we eliminated premade soup bases and began making all our stocks from scratch. Then we started a lengthy process of combing through all our ingredients to ferret out the additives. We found that soy sauce often contains preservatives or MSG, so we searched far and wide to find a clean one. We eliminated Worcestershire sauce from our recipes, because we couldn't find one without MSG. We started buying fresh-squeezed lemon and lime juices, since the bottled versions contain preservatives.

We had to get rid of panko crumbs altogether; they contain trans fats and, yet again, MSG. Now we grind up day-old bread to coat risotto cakes or chicken breasts or to use as an ingredient in meatballs or meatloaf.

We had to do some work to change our sourcing for meat. We discovered that oftentimes meat, especially chicken, is pumped full of salt and chemicals to make it extra moist and enhance its flavor (Thanksgiving turkeys suffer in particular from this affliction). Now we get all our chickens from a high-quality producer that doesn't pretreat them, and brine them ourselves in-house. We've looked into our meat suppliers extensively, and only work with brands whose practices we're comfortable with.

Canned tuna is often packed in a "broth" of MSG to augment flavor, and polyphosphates to make the fish retain water and maintain its firm texture. So, we now use only canned tuna without any of these ingredients.

All in all, I'm immensely proud of what we've built at Pasta & Co and the quality that we deliver to our customers. But our work is never done; we're constantly reworking our supplier relationships to get at the best, purest ingredients possible. Prawns and shrimp remain one of our biggest challenges. Our customers love these seafood items and we are forever looking for cleaner sources for them. For the most part, shrimp and prawns are imported from farms in Southeast Asia, where they are tended to by slave labor; they're then treated with sodium tripolyphosphate (which also happens to be an ingredient in laundry detergent) to pump up their moisture content. Once shipped to the U.S., they are scantly inspected by the FDA. Until the FDA makes it mandatory for fish distributors to disclose the additives they use to treat their catch, we can have little confidence in the purity of what we're eating.

ROASTED PARSNIPS,
ONIONS, AND
CAULIFLOWER

Vegetables

# ROASTED ONIONS

*(As seen on page 192-193)* Roasting works well with any variety of onion: sweet, red, yellow, or white. Spread them evenly on a baking sheet, without overlapping, to help them brown evenly and develop some char, then use the finished product anywhere you might use cooked onions (tossed with other vegetables, in salads, or on sandwiches). I use them all the time, including in my **BEEF AND MUSHROOM LASAGNA** (page 105).

**MAKES 1 POUND**

1 1/3 pounds red or yellow onions, peeled, trimmed of excess roots, and cut into 1/2-inch slices through the poles, leaving root end attachment intact, which makes the slices look like fans (about 2 onions)
1/2 teaspoon kosher salt
1/4 teaspoon black pepper
2 tablespoons expeller-pressed safflower oil

Preheat the oven to 450 degrees. In a large bowl, toss the onions with the salt, pepper, and oil. Spread the onions evenly on a baking sheet. Roast until softened and blackened in spots, 10 to 15 minutes.

# ROASTED FENNEL

Roasting fennel makes it both sweeter and more savory. Spread the pieces evenly on the baking sheet to ensure that they brown evenly and develop some char. When trimming the fennel, feel free to dice and use the stalks as well. Use this fennel tossed with other vegetables, in a salad, on a sandwich, or on its own as a side.

**SERVES 4
AS A SIDE DISH**

1 1/3 pounds fennel bulbs (about 1 large or 2 small), chopped into 1-inch pieces
1/2 teaspoon kosher salt
1/4 teaspoon black pepper
2 tablespoons expeller-pressed safflower oil

Preheat the oven to 425 degrees. In a large bowl, toss the fennel with the salt, pepper, and oil. Spread the fennel pieces evenly on a baking sheet, making sure they are not touching. Roast until softened and blackened in spots, 20 to 25 minutes.

# ROASTED PARSNIPS

*(As seen on page 192-193)* Parsnips are not very tasty raw, but they're great roasted. The really large ones sometimes have a woody core that needs to be discarded, especially when purchased in the summer months. Parsnips are irregular in shape, making them difficult to cut into uniform pieces. Don't worry as much about getting the pieces the same shape as the same approximate size, which is what will determine whether all the pieces are done at the same time. We use high heat here to achieve browning before the parsnips lose their texture. Be careful not to overcook them, because they quickly turn to mush and their high sugar content makes them susceptible to burning.

**MAKES 3/4 POUND**

1 pound parsnips (about 4 parsnips), cut into 2 x 1/2-inch pieces
1/4 teaspoon kosher salt
1/8 teaspoon black pepper
1 tablespoon expeller-pressed safflower oil

Preheat the oven to 450 degrees. In a large bowl, toss the parsnips with the salt, pepper, and oil. Spread the parsnip pieces evenly on a baking sheet, making sure they are not touching. Roast until softened and blackened in spots, 15 to 20 minutes.

# ROASTED BRUSSELS SPROUTS

Roasting Brussels sprouts changes them from the slimy, reviled food of our childhoods to pure nutty, crispy deliciousness. Out-of-season Brussels sprouts tend to have an off flavor, so avoid the temptation to make them during the warmer months from April through September. For an extra delicious touch, toss hot roasted Brussels sprouts with **NUTTY CHEESY BREADCRUMBS** (page 75) before serving.

**SERVES 8**

2 pounds Brussels sprouts, cut in half if larger than 1 inch in diameter
1/2 teaspoon kosher salt
1/4 teaspoon black pepper
2 tablespoons expeller-pressed safflower oil

Preheat the oven to 500 degrees. In a large bowl, toss the Brussels sprouts with the salt, pepper, and oil. Spread the Brussels sprouts evenly on a baking sheet, cut side down, making sure they are not touching. Roast until softened and blackened in spots, 20 to 25 minutes.

# ROASTED CAULIFLOWER

*(As seen on page 192-193)* Cauliflower is one of my favorite vegetables (second only to fennel). Roasting and browning it is the best way to maximize its flavor and optimize its texture. A little **THE BUTCHER'S TABLE SEASONING BLEND** (page 63) makes it extra savory.

**SERVES 4 TO 6**

1 head cauliflower, trimmed and cut into eighths, leaving core intact
1 1/2 tablespoons The Butcher's Table Seasoning Blend (page 63)
1 tablespoon drained capers, smashed and roughly chopped
1 teaspoon orange zest (1/2 orange)
1/2 teaspoon black pepper
1/2 cup expeller-pressed safflower oil

1. Preheat the oven to 425 degrees.

2. Place the cauliflower in a large bowl.

3. In a medium bowl, mix together The Butcher's Table Seasoning Blend, capers, orange zest, pepper, and oil until well combined. Pour the marinade mixture over the cauliflower and toss until the cauliflower is thoroughly coated. Place the cauliflower on a baking sheet, cut side down. Scrape any remaining marinade mixture from the large bowl onto the tops of the cauliflower pieces.

4. Roast in the oven until the cauliflower is browned and tender, 20 to 30 minutes.

---

### PRO TIP

For a heartier dish, top each piece of roasted cauliflower with a piece of Beecher's Dutch Hollow Dulcet cheese and return them to the oven to cook just until the cheese melts.

# ANCHO ROASTED CARROTS

*(As seen on page 198)* This rustic puree of roasted carrots and earthy ancho chile has a fair amount of tang, thanks to the addition of vinegar. I like to serve it as an accompaniment to meat, especially poultry, but it also works well as a spread for sandwiches or a dip for fresh vegetables.

**MAKES 2 1/2 CUPS,
SERVES 4 TO 6**

1 pound roughly chopped carrots (about 3 1/2 cups)
1/4 cup plus 1 tablespoon expeller-pressed safflower oil, divided
1 teaspoon plus a pinch of kosher salt, divided
Pinch of black pepper
2 cloves Roasted Garlic (page 76)
1/2 ancho chile, seeded and finely chopped
1/2 cup Chicken Stock (page 149)
1/4 cup white vinegar

1. Preheat the oven to 450 degrees.

2. In a large bowl, toss the carrots with 1 tablespoon of the oil, a pinch of salt, and pepper, and spread evenly on a baking sheet. Roast until browned all over and black in spots, 20 to 30 minutes. Set aside and let cool.

3. Meanwhile, in a food processor, combine the garlic, ancho chile, remaining 1 teaspoon salt, stock, and vinegar, and set aside to soften the chile while the carrots finish roasting and cool to room temperature, at least 5 minutes.

4. Process the chile mixture until mostly smooth. Add the carrots and remaining 1/4 cup oil, and pulse into a chunky puree. Store in an airtight container in the refrigerator for up to 3 days.

This is really good
Come on, try it!

WITH ANCHO
ROASTED CARROTS

# OVEN-BRAISED FENNEL

Fennel is my absolute favorite vegetable. It's so versatile and has a truly unique flavor that complements, without dominating, so many other ingredients. When roasted or braised, it's rich enough to stand up well to a wide variety of proteins. Turmeric lends this dish an earthiness, but more importantly, a vivid golden color that visually complements meat dishes. This braise makes an excellent side for everything from grilled sausages to poached fish, but pairs especially well with **OLD BAY ROASTED TURKEY BREAST** (page 138).

**SERVES 4 TO 6 AS A SIDE DISH**

1/2 teaspoon kosher salt
1/4 teaspoon ground turmeric
1/8 teaspoon black pepper
2 tablespoons extra-virgin olive oil
2 fennel bulbs, stalks trimmed, bulbs cut in half lengthwise
   and each half cut into 4 or 5 wedges, leaving the core intact

**1.** Preheat the oven to 400 degrees.

**2.** In a medium bowl, whisk together the salt, turmeric, pepper, and oil. Add the fennel and toss well to fully coat with the dressing. Transfer the fennel and the dressing to a rimmed baking sheet. Cover with foil and bake for 15 minutes, until the fennel is mostly tender.

**3.** Remove the foil and continue cooking until any liquid evaporates and the fennel begins to brown in spots, about 10 minutes.

Vegetables

# ROASTED RED PEPPER ANTIPASTI SPREAD

Serve this spread as a crostini topping, a pizza or pasta sauce, or an accompaniment for grilled vegetables and meats. If you already have **ROASTED RED PEPPERS** (page 214) and **ROASTED ONIONS** (page 194) on hand, this recipe comes together in a flash. I prefer using sweet onions here instead of the standard yellow onions to achieve the ideal salty, sour, sweet balance.

**MAKES ABOUT 3 CUPS**

3 red Fresno chiles
2 recipes Roasted Red Peppers (page 214)
2 recipes Roasted Onions (page 194; use sweet onions)
10 kalamata olives, pitted
1 tablespoon drained capers
4 tablespoons extra-virgin olive oil
2 tablespoons sherry vinegar

**1.** Using tongs and a gas burner (or in the oven, see note), roast the chiles, turning occasionally, until the skin is blistered all over and charred in spots. When cool enough to handle, remove the stems and seeds, leaving the skin on.

**2.** Combine the chiles and remaining ingredients in the bowl of a food processor and pulse until finely chopped (like the texture of a pickle relish).

**NOTE:**

If you don't have a gas burner, preheat the oven to 500 degrees. Toss the chiles with 1 to 2 teaspoons expeller-pressed safflower oil to lightly coat and place on a baking sheet. Roast until the skin is blistered all over and blackened in spots, 6 to 10 minutes.

# SPICY CHICKPEA PUREE

This recipe does triple duty as a spread, dip, or side dish. Consider serving it first as a side with **OLD BAY ROASTED TURKEY BREAST** (page 138) and using the leftovers throughout the remainder of the week as a dip for crudités and a spread for toast or sandwiches. It has a big leg up on store-bought hummus, which often contains added sugar as well as preservatives like citric acid and potassium sorbate.

**MAKES ABOUT 6 CUPS**

2 (15-ounce) cans chickpeas, drained with half of the liquid reserved
3 ounces Beecher's Smoked Flagship cheese (page 66 for alternate), roughly chopped (about 3/4 cup)
1/2 cup extra-virgin olive oil
6 tablespoons Red Fresno Sriracha (page 67)
1 tablespoon red wine vinegar
1/2 cup roughly chopped fresh cilantro

Combine the chickpeas, reserved liquid, cheese, oil, sriracha, and vinegar in a food processor and puree until the mixture is chunky. Add the cilantro and pulse until just combined.

# RED CABBAGE PEPERONATA

This peperonata is simultaneously sweet and sour, making it the perfect counterpoint to rich dishes. Supplementing the sweet peppers traditionally found in a peperonata with red cabbage increases the dish's visual and textural appeal. Consider serving it as part of an antipasto spread, or as a condiment for meats and salads. It is also a key ingredient in my **PAC 8 BROWN RICE SALAD** (page 187), **BEEF AND PEPERONATA CROSTINI** (page 100), and **FRENCH DIP ROAST BEEF SANDWICH WITH AU JUS** (page 96). It's best made at least a couple of hours in advance and can be stored in the refrigerator for up to a week.

**MAKES 4 1/2 CUPS**

3 medium cloves garlic, smashed and roughly chopped (about 1 1/2 tablespoons)
1 teaspoon kosher salt
1 teaspoon dried oregano
1/2 teaspoon red pepper flakes
1/2 teaspoon black pepper
1/3 cup plus 1 tablespoon expeller-pressed safflower oil, divided
1 pound mini sweet peppers, roughly chopped on the bias into 1-inch pieces (about 4 cups)
6 tablespoons white balsamic vinegar, divided
1/4 head red cabbage, cored and roughly chopped into 1-inch pieces (about 2 cups)

1. In a large bowl, combine the garlic, salt, oregano, red pepper flakes, and black pepper. Set aside.

2. In a large skillet over high heat, heat 1/3 cup of the oil just until smoking. Add the peppers. Stir the mixture once to coat with the oil, then let cook without stirring until the peppers begin to brown, about 3 minutes. Stir again and cook the peppers for 1 more minute. Add 3 tablespoons of the vinegar and cook for about 1 minute, reducing the liquid without overcooking the peppers. Transfer the peppers to the bowl with the garlic mixture.

3. Return the skillet to high heat and add the remaining 1 tablespoon oil, heating the oil just until smoking. Add the cabbage and stir to coat. Let cook without stirring until some of the cabbage begins to brown, about 2 minutes. Stir again and cook the cabbage for 1 more minute. Add the remaining 3 tablespoons vinegar and cook for about 1 minute, reducing the liquid without overcooking the cabbage. Transfer the cabbage to the bowl with the peppers and garlic mixture.

4. Stir well and cool to room temperature before serving or storing. The peperonata keeps for up to 1 week in an airtight container in the refrigerator.

# PURPLE POTATO SALAD WITH PEA VINES

A tangy vinaigrette and sweet pea vines make this potato salad lighter and more salad-y than classic versions. I like to use a combination of purple- and red-skinned potatoes for visual interest. If your potatoes are on the larger side, consider cutting them in half or quarters before slicing them 1/2 inch thick. Pea vines (sometimes called greens or shoots) are available in most Asian markets and some grocery stores during the spring. The mild, sweet flavor and crunchy stems are well worth the effort of seeking them out. If you can't find them, substitute spinach.

**SERVES 8**

1/3 cup plus 3 tablespoons extra-virgin olive oil, divided
1 1/4 pounds sweet onions (about 2 medium onions), chopped
3 pounds mixed purple- and red-skinned potatoes, halved and then cut into 1/2-inch slices
3 tablespoons kosher salt, divided
7 tablespoons cider vinegar, divided
10 cups water
2 teaspoons grainy mustard
1/2 teaspoon black pepper
5 ounces pea vines, roughly chopped
1/3 cup pitted and chopped kalamata olives
1/3 cup thinly sliced scallion (about 3 medium-size scallions)
1 red Fresno chile, seeded and diced

1. In a large skillet over medium-high heat, heat 3 tablespoons of the oil until shimmering, 1 to 2 minutes. Add the onions and stir to coat. Cook, stirring occasionally, until the onions soften and release some moisture, about 5 minutes. Reduce the heat to medium-low and cook, stirring frequently, until the onions are deeply browned and slightly sticky, 30 to 40 minutes longer. (If the onions are sizzling or scorching, reduce the heat. If the onions are not browning after 15 to 20 minutes, raise the heat.) Set aside.

2. Meanwhile, in a large pot over high heat, bring the potatoes, 2 tablespoons of the salt, 2 tablespoons of the vinegar, and the water to a boil.

Reduce the heat to medium and simmer until the potatoes are just tender, 15 to 20 minutes.

3. While the potatoes are cooking, mix together the grainy mustard, remaining 1 tablespoon salt, pepper, remaining 5 tablespoons vinegar, and remaining 1/3 cup oil in a large bowl. When the potatoes are tender, drain and add immediately to the large bowl with the dressing. Gently stir to coat. When the potatoes have cooled, toss with the caramelized onions, pea vines, kalamata olives, scallion, and chile, and serve. (The salad can be refrigerated in an airtight container for 1 to 3 days.)

Vegetables

205

# ROASTED MUSHROOM SALAD WITH BABY KALE

**ROASTED MUSHROOMS** (page 215) are packed with more flavor than almost any other vegetarian item. When combined with ultra-savory Beecher's Smoked Flagship cheese in a salad of hearty kale and fennel, you have the recipe for a memorable vegetarian entrée or a healthy counterpoint to a grilled steak. Piquillo peppers and **QUICK PICKLED RED ONIONS** (page 84) add a colorful pop and zesty brightness to this hearty salad.

**SERVES 4**

1 recipe Roasted Mushrooms (page 215)

5 ounces baby kale (see note), roughly chopped

1/2 recipe Quick Pickled Red Onions (page 84), drained and roughly chopped (about 1/2 cup)

1/2 fennel bulb, halved and thinly sliced or shaved on a mandoline

4 jarred piquillo peppers, sliced (about 1/2 cup)

6 ounces Beecher's Smoked Flagship cheese (page 66 for alternate), coarsely grated (about 1 1/2 cups)

Kosher salt and black pepper, to taste

In a large bowl, toss the mushrooms, kale, onions, fennel, and peppers until thoroughly mixed. Gently fold in the cheese. Add salt and pepper to taste. Serve immediately.

**NOTE:**

If you can't find baby kale, substitute mature kale cut into thick ribbons (aka chiffonade).

# SMASHED POTATOES

This is my go-to potato side dish, especially for steaks. Smashed potatoes are the perfect compromise between fried and mashed potatoes, delivering both crispy and creamy textures. Once the potatoes are par-cooked, the dish comes together quickly just before mealtime.

**SERVES 4 TO 6**

2 1/2 pounds red potatoes, 2 to 3 inches in diameter
6 tablespoons butter, divided
1 large shallot, diced (about 1/2 cup)
2 tablespoons capers, drained
2 teaspoons kosher salt
1 teaspoon smoked paprika
1/2 cup thinly shaved red cabbage
2/3 cup roughly chopped fresh flat-leaf parsley leaves

**1.** Cook the potatoes whole in the microwave until tender and the flesh shrinks away from the skin, 15 to 25 minutes (rotating every 5 minutes). Flatten each potato to a 1/2-inch thickness and roughly chop into bite-size pieces.

**2.** In a large skillet over medium heat, melt 4 tablespoons of the butter. Add the shallot, capers, salt, and paprika and cook until fragrant, about 1 minute. Add the potatoes and stir to coat evenly with the butter mixture. Cook, without stirring, until the potatoes are browned on the bottom side, 3 to 5 minutes. Stir and cook for another 3 to 5 minutes, stirring occasionally. Add the cabbage and remaining 2 tablespoons butter and cook, stirring occasionally, until the potatoes are browned all over, another 3 to 5 minutes.

**3.** Transfer the potato mixture to a large bowl and fold in the parsley until the parsley is evenly distributed. Serve immediately.

### PRO TIP

Leftover potatoes can be rewarmed in a skillet.

# SHAVED ASPARAGUS SALAD

Asparagus is sweeter left raw than cooked, and works nicely as the basis of a springtime salad. Use a mandoline slicer, a peeler, or a sharp knife to create long, thin, irregular shavings of the asparagus and carrot. Try standing your asparagus on an upside-down bowl as you shave it with a peeler. Don't worry if the pieces aren't uniform. In fact, a little variety gives the salad better body and volume—like a shag haircut! Serve garnished with **CRISP PROSCIUTTO** (page 84), grated Beecher's Flagship Reserve cheese (page 66 for alternate), or **NUTTY CHEESY BREADCRUMBS** (page 75).

**SERVES 6
AS A SIDE OR
STARTER SALAD**

2 tablespoons expeller-pressed safflower oil

2 tablespoons seasoned rice vinegar

2 tablespoons lemon juice

Kosher salt, to taste

Pinch of black pepper

1 1/2 pounds asparagus, tough ends snapped off, shaved or sliced into 2- to 3-inch-long ribbons on the bias (about 1 bunch)

2 ounces arugula (about 2 cups packed)

2 scallions, cut in half lengthwise and roughly chopped

1/2 carrot, shaved into 2- to 3-inch-long ribbons

1 ounce hazelnuts, chopped (3 tablespoons), divided

**1.** To make the dressing, in a medium bowl, whisk together the oil, vinegar, lemon juice, salt, and pepper.

**2.** In a large bowl, toss together the asparagus, arugula, scallions, carrots, and half of the hazelnuts.

**3.** Just before serving, toss the salad mixture with the dressing and serve, topped with the remaining hazelnuts. Season with additional salt and pepper to taste.

# CONFETTI GRATIN

This gratin recipe is streamlined and easy. Beecher's rich Flagship cheese does the job of both the cream and the cheese called for in the typical gratin recipe. The addition of corn flour ensures that the melted cheese doesn't break and turn stringy. When purchasing potatoes, select a variety of colors so that the dish lives up to its "confetti" name. I recommend purple-, pink-, and red-skinned varieties, in addition to white potatoes. Choose larger potatoes, as they are easier to grate.

This dish really does not work well without an extra-coarse grater to grate the potatoes. My favorite is the 11-inch stainless steel tower grater by Progressive, available on Amazon (see page 53 for more information). It's a good tool. Buy it! Serve garnished with **CRISP PROSCIUTTO** (page 84), grated Beecher's Flagship Reserve cheese (page 66 for alternate), or **NUTTY CHEESY BREADCRUMBS** (page 75).

**SERVES 6 TO 8
AS A SIDE DISH**

2 1/4 pounds multicolored unpeeled potatoes, coarsely grated
1 tablespoon lemon juice
12 ounces Beecher's Flagship cheese (page 66 for alternate), coarsely grated (3 cups)
1/2 medium yellow onion, coarsely grated
1/2 red bell pepper, coarsely grated or roughly chopped
3 tablespoons corn flour
2 tablespoons roughly chopped fresh thyme
2 tablespoons roughly chopped fresh flat-leaf parsley
1 1/2 teaspoons kosher salt
1 teaspoon granulated garlic
1/2 teaspoon black pepper

**1.** Preheat the oven to 400 degrees. Butter a 9 x 13-inch glass or ceramic baking dish.

**2.** In a large bowl, toss the potatoes with the lemon juice immediately upon grating, to prevent browning. To the bowl, add the cheese, onion, bell pepper, corn flour, thyme, parsley, salt, garlic, and black pepper.

**3.** Spread the mixture evenly into the dish and press down lightly, making sure the vegetables are not sticking up. Bake for 45 to 55 minutes, until the dish is fully browned on top. Let cool for 10 minutes before serving.

# BUTTERNUT SQUASH MASH

Serve this simple side dish just as you would mashed potatoes (which have their moments, but I find to be generally bland and low on redeeming nutritional qualities). Sweet butternut squash makes an especially good counterpoint to savory **BRAISED BEEF CHUCK ROAST** (page 102), or anything else that's rich or robustly flavored. Unlike mashed potatoes, squash does not stiffen or become gluey when cooled. That means it can be made ahead and reheated when you're ready to serve it.

**SERVES 4 TO 6
AS A SIDE DISH**

1 butternut squash, cut in half lengthwise and seeded (about 3 pounds)
2 teaspoons expeller-pressed safflower oil
1 1/2 teaspoons kosher salt
1/4 teaspoon black pepper
2 tablespoons unsalted butter
1 teaspoon apple cider vinegar

**1.** Preheat the oven to 375 degrees.

**2.** Brush the cut surfaces of the squash with the oil. Place both halves cut side down on a baking sheet. Roast until very tender, about 60 minutes. Remove from the oven and let rest for 10 minutes, or until the squash is cool enough to handle.

**3.** Using a spoon, transfer the flesh to a medium bowl, discarding the skin. Using a fork, potato masher, or whisk, mash the squash with the salt, pepper, butter, and vinegar until mostly smooth. Serve immediately or make up to a few days ahead and rewarm to serve.

**NOTE:**
To brown the butter, melt it in a skillet over medium heat. Continue cooking, stirring frequently with a spatula, until the foaming subsides, the solids turn deep brown, and the aroma is toasty, about 3 minutes. Immediately pour the finished browned butter out of the hot skillet to halt the cooking and prevent burning.

> ### PRO TIP
>
> ........................................
>
> As is, the dish is a great "backup singer," which is sometimes exactly what you want in a side dish. To make it more of a "diva," double and/or brown the butter (see note) and add 1/2 teaspoon orange zest and 2 teaspoons brown sugar.

# WILTED COLLARD GREENS

Collard greens get a bad rap because many old-fashioned recipes cook them for hours until army green and mushy. Here, gently wilted collards maintain their vibrant color and toothsome texture. Unlike typical preparations, where the stems are discarded, this recipe makes use of them as a crisp textural counterpoint to the tender leaves. The sweet onions and acidic vinegar balance the natural bitterness of the collards and make this healthy side memorable.

These greens are best served immediately after cooking. Consider making the vinegar mixture up to an hour before mealtime, then cooking the greens just as you are sitting down to eat.

**SERVES 6**

1 pound collard greens
2 tablespoons expeller-pressed safflower oil
1/2 red onion, chopped (about 1/2 cup)
1 teaspoon kosher salt
3 tablespoons apple cider vinegar

**1.** Strip the collard green leaves from the stems, reserving the stems. Roughly chop the leaves into 2-inch squares. Trim the bottom inch from the stems and discard. Chop the remaining stems into 1/4-inch pieces.

**2.** In a large skillet over medium heat, heat the oil until shimmering. Add the onion and salt and cook, stirring occasionally, until the onions are fully translucent and beginning to brown, about 5 minutes. Add the vinegar and cook until the mixture is reduced by half, about 2 minutes. If not serving immediately, remove the skillet from the heat and set aside until mealtime.

**3.** At mealtime, return the skillet containing the onion and vinegar mixture to medium-high heat. Add the collard stems and cook for 1 to 2 minutes, until they turn a vibrant green. Add the leaves and cook, mixing frequently with tongs, for 1 to 2 minutes, until the leaves are wilted and vibrant green. Serve immediately.

> ### PRO TIP
>
> ..............................................
>
> For extra flavor, use rendered pork lard (see page 132) instead of safflower oil.

*Really any winter greens could work here. Or a mixture.*

# ROASTED RED PEPPERS

*(As seen on page 224–225)* It's incredible how dramatically roasting transforms the taste of red peppers. Their flavor changes from grassy, fresh, and vegetal to something truly rich and sweet in a matter of minutes. Be sure to let them blister and char thoroughly before removing them from the heat; not only will any skin left raw stick stubbornly to the pepper, but also the taste just won't be the same if left even a little bit undercooked.

**MAKES ABOUT 1 CUP**　　　1 red bell pepper (about 8 ounces)

Using tongs and a gas burner, roast the pepper, turning occasionally, until the skin is blistered all over and charred in spots. If you don't have a gas burner, preheat the oven to 500 degrees. Toss the pepper with 1 teaspoon expeller-pressed safflower oil to lightly coat and place on a baking sheet. Roast until the skin is blistered all over and blackened in spots, about 15 minutes. Place the roasted pepper in a covered bowl or sealed bag to steam and cool. When cool enough to handle, remove the skin, stem, and seeds and slice into 1/4-inch slices.

# ROASTED TURNIPS

Turnips are like the straight-to-video equivalent of the vegetable world; basically inedible raw, but roasted and tossed with other roasted vegetables, they can play a satisfying role. Be careful not to overcook them, because they will quickly turn to mush.

**MAKES 3/4 POUND**
1 pound turnips (about 3 turnips), cut in half and sliced
　　into 3/4-inch-thick wedges
1/4 teaspoon kosher salt
1/8 teaspoon black pepper
1 tablespoon expeller-pressed safflower oil

Preheat the oven to 450 degrees. In a large bowl, toss the turnips with the salt, pepper, and oil. Spread the turnip pieces evenly on a baking sheet, making sure they are not touching. Roast until softened and browned in spots, 18 to 25 minutes.

# ROASTED MUSHROOMS

For the most robust flavor, I suggest using portobello mushrooms. However, creminis (cut in half) can be substituted for a milder flavor. **THE BUTCHER'S TABLE SEASONING BLEND** (page 63) really shines in this recipe. Roasting transforms the mushrooms into vegetarian umami bombs, and this savory seasoning blend amplifies their meatiness. Use these to top salads, fill omelets, or as a vegetarian substitute any time you might use leftover cooked beef. These mushrooms are also the base for the **BEEF AND MUSHROOM LASAGNA** (page 105) and **WINTER PESTO** (page 91).

**MAKES 10 OUNCES**

1 tablespoon The Butcher's Table Seasoning Blend (page 63)
1/2 teaspoon kosher salt
1/4 teaspoon black pepper
2 tablespoons expeller-pressed safflower oil
1 tablespoon balsamic vinegar
1 pound portobello mushrooms (about 4)

**1.** Preheat the oven to 450 degrees.

**2.** In a large bowl, whisk together The Butcher's Table Seasoning Blend, salt, pepper, oil, and vinegar.

**3.** Cut the mushrooms in half and then cut each half in half again. Toss the mushrooms with the vinegar mixture until as evenly distributed as possible. (The vinegar mixture will not fully coat the mushrooms.)

**4.** Spread the mushrooms evenly on a baking sheet, making sure they are not touching. Roast until softened and browned on the exterior, 15 to 20 minutes, rotating the pan after 12 minutes.

QUICK & EASY

COOKIES

Sweets

# QUICK & EASY COOKIES

*(As seen on page 216–217)* Levain Bakery on the Upper West Side makes some of the most sought-after cookies in all of New York City. They are different from your typical cookie and remind me of a cross between a cookie and a scone, with a crunchy exterior and a soft interior. This recipe mimics the texture of Levain's cookies but without the use of flour. The "dump and stir" method and "use whatever you have on hand" ingredient list makes this the perfect recipe for when it's 9:30 p.m. and you've just gotta have a cookie. My favorite variation includes peanut butter, apples, granola, dried cranberries, and a sprinkling of Maldon salt, but feel free to come up with your own creative combinations.

**MAKES 12 COOKIES**

1 cup salted nut butter (peanut, almond, or cashew; see note)
1 cup add-ins (a mixture of the following): chocolate chips, dried fruit, nuts, granola, oats, seeds
1/2 cup packed brown sugar
1/2 cup small diced apple or pear pieces (about 1/2 medium apple or pear, cored, but unpeeled)
2 eggs
1 teaspoon vanilla extract
1/2 teaspoon kosher salt

**1.** Preheat the oven to 350 degrees.

**2.** Mix all of the ingredients, except the salt, together in a medium bowl. Drop the dough onto parchment-lined baking sheets, sprinkle each cookie with salt, and bake until puffed and browned on the edges, 12 to 15 minutes, switching and rotating the sheets halfway through baking.

**3.** Let the cookies cool on the baking sheets for 2 minutes, then transfer to a wire rack and cool completely. (These cookies can be stored in an airtight container at room temperature for up to 3 days.)

**NOTE:**
Look for nut butters made from only nuts and salt and none of the hydrogenated oil, sugars, or additives that are often included. If you buy unsalted nut butter, add some salt to the cookie batter. If you buy nut butter with added sugar or your add-ins are particularly sweet, reduce the amount of brown sugar called for in the recipe.

I really like to minimize added sugar in my diet. These cookies have just enough sugar to give them a slight sweetness. If you have a serious sweet tooth, consider doubling the sugar.

# APPLE & PEAR CRISP

I like to make crisps for my family because they're forgiving to cook as desserts go, and work well with a variety of fruits. We tend to keep apples and pears around at all times for eating out of hand. When our fruit bowl starts overflowing, I make this crisp. Feel free to vary the proportion of apples and pears to your personal taste, or whatever you happen to have on hand. My favorite apple varietals for crisps are Pink Lady and Honeycrisp. Most baked apple recipes call for peeling, but I try not to peel any of my fruits or vegetables because it saves time and preserves nutrition, and I like the added texture.

**SERVES 8 TO 10**

**FOR THE FILLING:**
4 crisp apples, cored and diced large
   (about 1 3/4 pounds)
3 pears, cored and diced large
   (about 1 1/2 pounds)
1/4 cup brown sugar
1/2 teaspoon ground ginger
1/4 teaspoon kosher salt
1 tablespoon lemon juice
1/4 teaspoon lemon zest
   (about 1/2 lemon)
1 teaspoon vanilla extract
4 tablespoons unsalted butter,
   cut into 12 pieces

**FOR THE TOPPING:**
1 cup packed brown sugar
3/4 cup old-fashioned oats
3/4 cup pecans
1/2 cup unsalted butter,
   cut into 8 pieces
1/2 cup whole wheat pastry flour
1/2 teaspoon kosher salt
1/4 teaspoon cinnamon
1/8 teaspoon cardamom

1. Preheat the oven to 400 degrees.

2. To make the filling, in a large bowl, mix together the apples, pears, brown sugar, ginger, salt, lemon juice, zest, and vanilla until combined. Transfer the mixture to a 9 x 13-inch glass or ceramic baking dish. Top with the butter pieces.

3. To make the topping, pulse all of the ingredients together in a food processor until the mixture has the texture of coarse crumbs (with some pea-size pieces of butter remaining). Scatter the topping evenly over the filling and bake until the juices are bubbling and the topping is deep golden brown, 35 to 45 minutes. (If the topping is browning too quickly, loosely cover with a piece of aluminum foil.)

4. Transfer to a wire rack to cool for at least 15 minutes. Serve warm.

# BEECHER'S NO-BAKE SUPER-LIGHT CHEESECAKE

This cheesecake is easy to make and doesn't require any esoteric tools or pans. Instead of using the standard cream cheese, this recipe combines the full flavor of Beecher's Flagship cheese with creamy mascarpone. I like to coarsely grate the cheese so that I can taste it distinctly within the cheesecake. If you can't find Beecher's crackers, and don't want to buy them online, feel free to substitute an equal quantity of any lightly sweetened, all-natural, whole wheat cracker. The crust can be made ahead, baked, cooled, and stored wrapped in airtight plastic wrap for 24 hours. The filled, sauced dessert can be made up to 24 hours in advance and stored in the refrigerator, then garnished with fresh raspberries just before serving.

**FOR THE CRUST:**
1 (5-ounce) bag Beecher's Honey Hazelnut Crackers
4 tablespoons brown sugar
5 tablespoons unsalted butter, melted

**FOR THE FILLING:**
1 teaspoon gelatin
1/4 cup lemon juice (1 to 2 lemons)
12 ounces mascarpone cheese
1/2 cup plus 2 tablespoons confectioners' sugar, divided
1 cup heavy cream
6 ounces Beecher's Flagship cheese (page 66 for alternate),
    coarsely grated (about 1 1/2 cups)

**SERVES 8**

**FOR THE TOPPING:**
1/2 teaspoon gelatin
1 teaspoon lemon juice
18 ounces raspberries (about 3 small clamshells), divided
5 tablespoons brown sugar
Pinch of kosher salt

1. To make the crust, adjust the oven rack to the middle position and heat the oven to 350 degrees. In a food processor, process the crackers and sugar to fine, even crumbs, about 30 seconds. Add the melted butter in a steady stream while pulsing; pulse until the mixture is evenly moistened and sticks together when pressed between your fingers. >>

Transfer the mixture to a 9-inch pie pan. Using the bottom of a dry measuring cup, press the cracker mixture firmly and evenly into the pan bottom and up the sides. Use the back of a spoon to make an even edge. Bake until fragrant and golden brown, 12 to 18 minutes. Cool on a wire rack to room temperature, about 30 minutes. Set aside to cool completely.

2. To make the filling, while the crust is cooling, sprinkle the gelatin evenly over the surface of the lemon juice in a small micro-wave-safe bowl and set aside 5 to 10 minutes. Heat the gelatin mixture in the microwave for 30 seconds, or until steaming. Set aside to cool to room temperature. In a large bowl, mix the mascarpone and 1/2 cup of the confectioners' sugar with a spatula. In a separate large bowl, whisk the cream and remaining 2 tablespoons confectioners' sugar until soft peaks form, 3 to 5 minutes, and set aside. Stir the cooled gelatin mixture into the mascarpone mixture. Stir the grated cheese into the mascarpone mixture. Gently fold the whipped cream into the mascarpone cheese mixture. Transfer the filling to the cooled crust. Using a spoon, spread the filling to the outer edges to create an indentation in the middle with a 1-inch lip around the edges. Place in the refrigerator for at least 2 hours to set.

3. To make the topping, sprinkle the gelatin evenly over the surface of the lemon juice and set aside for 5 to 10 minutes. In a medium skillet over medium-high heat, combine two-thirds of the raspberries with the sugar and salt, mashing lightly with a spatula. Cook, stirring occasionally, until thickened and the spatula leaves a trail when drawn across the bottom of the pan, about 10 minutes. Stir in the gelatin mixture and transfer to a small bowl to cool to room temperature. Pour the cooled sauce into the indentation in the filling on the surface of the pie. Return the pie to the refrigerator for at least 30 minutes or until ready to serve.

4. Just before serving, place the remaining raspberries in the built-up filling border around the edge of pie.

# CURRIED HAZELNUTS AND CHOCOLATE BARK

I prefer a mixture of dark and semisweet chocolate, but you can use whatever chocolate you wish.

**MAKES ABOUT 16 PIECES**

12 ounces dark chocolate (about 70% cacao)
4 ounces semisweet chocolate (about 40% cacao)
1 1/2 cups Lura's Curried Hazelnuts (page 88), roughly chopped
Sea salt to taste

**1.** Using a double boiler, melt the chocolate. Alternatively, boil water in a pot, remove the pot from the heat, and place a heat-safe bowl over the pot. Add the chocolate to the bowl and stir until the chocolate is completely melted.

**2.** Line a baking sheet with parchment paper. Using a spatula, scrape the chocolate out of the bowl and onto the parchment, and then spread the chocolate out into a 1/8- to 1/4-inch layer that is roughly 8 x 12 inches.

**3.** Sprinkle the hazelnuts over the chocolate in one even layer. Lightly sprinkle with the salt and refrigerate, uncovered, for 20 minutes, or until the chocolate is firm. If your baking sheet does not fit into your refrigerator, you can set your baking sheet in a cool space and let set for 2 hours.

**4.** When the bark has cooled completely, invert the chocolate onto a cutting board and remove the parchment paper. Using the tip of a sharp knife, score the back of the chocolate with 3 parallel lines along the length and width. Flip the chocolate over and break along the scored lines.

**5.** The bark can be stored in the refrigerator for up to 2 weeks.

Appendices

Metric Conversions

| U.S. STANDARD | U.K. |
|---|---|
| 1/4 tsp | 1/4 tsp (scant) |
| 1/2 tsp | 1/2 tsp (scant) |
| 3/4 tsp | 1/2 tsp (rounded) |
| 1 tsp | 3/4 tsp (slightly rounded) |
| 1 tbsp | 2 1/2 tsp |
| 1/4 cup | 1/4 cup minus 1 dsp |
| 1/3 cup | 1/4 cup plus 1 tsp |
| 1/2 cup | 1/3 cup plus 2 dsp |
| 2/3 cup | 1/2 cup plus 1 dsp |
| 3/4 cup | 1/2 cup plus 2 tbsp |
| 1 cup | 3/4 cup plus 2 dsp |

**OVEN TEMPERATURES**

| Fahrenheit (F) | Celsius (C) |
|---|---|
| 250°F | 120°C |
| 275°F | 140°C |
| 300°F | 150°C |
| 325°F | 160°C |
| 350°F | 180°C |
| 375°F | 190°C |
| 400°F | 200°C |
| 425°F | 220°C |
| 450°F | 230°C |
| 475°F | 245°C |
| 500°F | 260°C |

# Further Reading

This book is intended to provide a basic, practical guide to eating pure. If you're interested in more in-depth exploration of the subject of food additives and processed food's takeover of America, below are some recommended books on the subject.

Lustig, Robert. *Fat Chance: Beating the Odds Against Sugar, Processed Food, Obesity, and Disease.* New York: Plume, 2013.

Moss, Michael. *Salt, Sugar, Fat: How the Food Giants Hooked Us.* New York: Random House, 2014.

Nestle, Marion. *What to Eat.* New York: North Point Press, 2007.

Pollan, Michael. *In Defense of Food: An Eater's Manifesto.* New York: Penguin, 2009.

—. *Food Rules: An Eater's Manual.* New York: Penguin, 2014.

—. *The Omnivore's Dilemma: A Natural History of Four Meals.* New York: Penguin, 2007.

Warner, Melanie. *Pandora's Lunchbox: How Processed Foods Took Over the American Meal.* New York: Scribner, 2013.

PAN-SEARED RIB-EYE WITH THE
BUTCHER'S TABLE SEASONING
BLEND, UPPER EAST SIDE STEAK
SAUCE, CHIMCHURRI

BEER-BRINED
CHICKEN WINGS
WITH RED FRESNO
SRIRACHA

# Index

Index

235

## KURT BEECHER DAMMEIER

A fourth generation Puget Sound native and nascent New Yorker, Kurt has always felt passionately about authentic, full-flavored foods free of artificial additives and preservatives. In 2000, he officially made his entrance onto the Seattle food scene by buying Pasta & Co, a Seattle icon for over thirty-five years. Since that time, he's opened and served as head chef at a number of Seattle food destinations under the Sugar Mountain umbrella, including Beecher's Handmade Cheese, Bennett's, Liam's, Maximus / Minimus, and The Butcher's Table. Sugar Mountain is also home to a line of premium meat products, including Mishima Reserve, a luxury Wagyu beef brand. With each operation, Kurt's goal is to demonstrate how quality ingredients make for delicious meals, without added food colorings, flavor enhancers, or preservatives. Beyond the retail world, Kurt is effecting change in people's eating habits through the Beecher's Pure Food Kids Foundation (501c3), founded through Beecher's in 2004. Each year, the foundation's Pure Food Kids Workshop empowers more than 15,000 fourth and fifth grade students in the Seattle Metro area and in New York City to make healthy food choices for life.

Commit yourself
to the simple goal of
avoiding additives.
The rest falls into place.